Endorsements

Craig Walker asks the big question, "What will you do with your life?"—and then challenges us to live extraordinary lives in God, making our lives count in the light of eternity. Not only does Craig challenge us, he shows us the way using the Word of God coupled with stirring personal testimonies. In Jesus, you too can be a world changer!

Dr. Michael L. Brown
Bestselling author
Host of The Line of Fire radio broadcast

Never before has there been a time in history better suited for the end-time harvest than today. Pastor Craig Walker has picked the lock of the prison doors where lost souls incarcerated in hell's darkest corners on earth have languished in hopelessness for centuries. Those who live in darkness have seen a glorious light! *Born for the Extraordinary* simply unveils the modern delivery system of the scrolls of His generation, utilizing current technology to deliver the same liberation message of life in Christ. The most timely book available on utilizing the communication advantages of this last generation. A must read.

Dave Roever

I have known Craig Walker for several decades. I was his and Lezli's pastor at Brownsville in Pensacola. I always knew Craig would become who he is today. He treasures the anointing. This new release, *Born for the Extraordinary*, is just that—it is anointed. Within the pages of this book there are keys that will unlock your sacred calling and realign your priorities.

Pastor John Kilpatrick
Church of His Presence

Born for the Extraordinary is a masterpiece. A must read for all believers. It will point you to your destiny, clarify your calling, and unlock your great potential. I have known Craig and his wife Lezli for the past 25 years and can say without a hint of reservation that they are the real deal. Craig is my dear friend, a fellow laborer in the harvest, and one who has touched thousands on GOD TV.

Ward Simpson
CEO, GOD TV

Born for the Extraordinary

Harrison House

Shippensburg, PA

Born for the Extraordinary

CRAIG WALKER

Published by Harrison House Publishers
Shippensburg, PA 17257

Cover design by Eileen Rockwell.

ISBN 13 TP: 978-1-6803-1715-2

ISBN 13 eBook: 978-1-6803-1716-9

ISBN 13 HC: 978-1-6803-1718-3

ISBN 13 LP: 978-1-6803-1717-6

For Worldwide Distribution, Printed in the U.S.A.

1 2 3 4 5 6 7 8 / 25 24 23 22 21

Acknowledgments

I wish to thank the late Dr. Vinson Synan for the life-changing prayer in his living room that placed a writer's anointing upon my life, and for his and Carol's cherished friendship.

I want to acknowledge two extraordinary sons in the faith, Joe Jr. and Vinny, for their willingness to take giants leaps of faith together with me.

I could never express all of my gratitude to Pastor John Kilpatrick for believing in Lezli and I at the beginning of our ministry life.

I want to honor the late Rev. Ken Sumrall who was a true father in the faith to us.

I want to honor my ninety-year-old father Rev. Ralph Walker Sr. who is a mighty man of faith and has successfully passed the faith of his fathers on to his children, my siblings, their spouses, and all of their children.

I want to thank our Upward Church intercessors who are the true heroes, and to the late Carolyn Ongalo who I can hear cheering us on from heaven shouting, "Come on Jesus!"

I want to tell my late brother-in-law Pastor Preston Pitchford, "We will meet you, brother, at the feet of Jesus and we are not coming empty handed!"

For all of the pastors, intercessors, and workers on the frontlines around the world, risking their lives for the Gospel, this book is your story. Pastor Noah, Gideon, Pastor John and Rachael, we shall plunder hell and populate heaven together!

For the folks at Harrison House and my book agent Karen Hardin, I am forever indebted to you.

For the Upward Church family and staff, we are the "little boy's lunch in the hands of a big God," and 100 Million souls is our portion. I am so grateful for you.

To my lovely children, Christian and Candace, you are my very joy, the apple of my eye. No father was ever prouder of his godly children.

And finally to my beautiful wife Lezli, you are my rock, the ever-praying supportive partner. Your diligent prayers have opened up so many doors. I never want to do life without you.

To all of you, and so many more, thank you! Thank you! Thank you!

For those who have never heard,

Contents

Follow the Breadcrumbs

AT the end of our lives, will we be able to proclaim with confidence that we lived the life we were destined to live? Will we have finally scratched the proverbial itch to find our real purpose? These questions are sometimes shelved and brushed aside when we are young, but in our later years they demand a truthful response. Young or old, we should do everything within our power to be able to say at the end of our days, "I accomplished all that I was placed here to do."

Hidden within scripture are covert clues that can direct us to this end. Our Creator left breadcrumbs along the path to help us find our specific purpose. This book will help you break that code and unlock your peak potential—to discover the best life you always wanted to live. The following is a roadmap to purpose, meaning, and joy.

THE FIRST CLUE

Our first clue is that we were born into this generation by God's appointment. The Bible says that, "*From one man he made all the nations, that they should inhabit the whole earth: and he marked out their appointed times in history and the boundaries of their lands"* (Acts 17:26). God placed each of us in the specific generation where our unique gifts and talents can make the greatest impact. We are not random DNA, nor are we randomly placed in time.

Israel's King David is an example of this truth. The Bible states that, *"When David had served God's purpose in his own generation, he fell asleep"* (Acts 13:36). He was placed in his generation by God's design. King David's highest potential was tailor-fitted for the generation in which he lived, and so is ours. The age in which we are born is immutably bound to our destiny. This is the first clue toward understanding our God-given destiny.

The age in which we are born is immutably bound to our destiny.

Because our highest potential is tied to our specific generation, a closer examination of our times will assist us in unraveling the mystery of His will for our lives. The present day is a world of accelerated technological advances that invade and daily alter our lifestyles in profound ways. For those alive today, every facet of life is influenced by technology. (Can you remember when we didn't have smartphones or internet banking?) Understanding the enormous role technology plays in our lives will help us discover our purpose. More will be said about this later.

THE SECOND CLUE

King David served God's purpose in his generation and then he died. These few words are a precise description of God's desire for every person in their respective generations. Whether we are cognizant of it or not, this is our true purpose in life. Deep within every child of God is a profound desire to fulfill this destiny.

The real challenge of life is to make David's eulogy our own. Standing in the way is the foreboding obstacle of self-doubt. It whispers that we don't have what it takes, or we are not qualified. One of the great ironies of life is that we coexist with a deep desire to do something extraordinary with our lives while feeling underqualified to do exceptional things. While the flames of passion roar within to make a lasting footprint, many outwardly struggle to understand their role, puzzled by what greatness could even look like for them. It is quite common to feel inadequate for the extraordinary things God wants to accomplish through us.

The struggle is real, but God's plan for our lives is never mediocre. His plan for every person is greatness! And while that destiny may as yet remain unclear, one thing is certain—unless we are willing to press in and push past our comfort zone, we will never achieve it. Significant risk is required to do significant things for God.

Significant risk is required to do significant things for God.

Right now, there is an unprecedented window of opportunity open for those who feel underqualified to do extraordinary things for God. I never imagined that God would allow me to witness in twenty months:

- Nearly 800,000 people coming to Christ.
- In a single night 153,249 people surrender to Christ in the middle of Pakistan during Ramadan.
- African witch doctors coming to Christ with two of them surrendering more than seventy innocent children who were to be human sacrifices.

You and I live in the greatest era of opportunity that mankind has ever known. Today's technology has unlocked a treasure chest full of opportunities for exponential influence and impact. This new season is fertile and packed full of possibility for those who will recognize the hour and seize the day.

Today's technology provides us with an opportunity to reach hundreds of thousands of people without obtaining a visa or demanding that we leave our own countries. Our destiny is bound to the generation in which we live.

We were all born with a preplanned itinerary. The Bible states, *"For we are God's handiwork, created in Christ Jesus to do good works, which God prepared in advance for us to do"* (Eph. 2:10). We often refer to this as "God's will for our lives." The only life truly worthy of our trips around the sun is the one found in the very center of His will.

Our Creator has stamped His watermark upon each of our lives. A watermark is a translucent design impressed on paper during manufacturing, invisible until the paper is held to the light. The potential to display our heavenly Father's watermark resides in each of us. It is illuminated by the light of Jesus.

The purpose of a watermark is to identify an original from a counterfeit. I bought a purse for my wife in Italy in an open square. The vendor assured me that is was made of the "highest quality genuine Italian leather." We wish it had a watermark on it of some kind so we could tell the real from the counterfeit. We still have nagging doubts that this purse is all it was promised to be. Have you ever felt that way about the life you are current living?

Every human comes with God's watermark, only visible when held in the light of Jesus. We are made in the image of God—each an original. If we choose a life without His mark on display, we are living a counterfeit version of what God has planned for us. A life of far less value. In this condition we are not living our God-given destiny. Only a small portion of His image is visible when walking outside of His design. Choosing our own path causes His image to be blurred. We remain merely semitransparent. It is difficult to see the Creator's design without His watermark illuminated. It is impossible to live the great adventure God preplanned for us when it is missing.

Jesus Christ is the Father's watermark—"*the exact representation of his being*" (Heb. 1:3). When our steps are squarely in the Father's will, Jesus shines through us. Your very best life is realized when His watermark is the most evident in you.

Just as photographers twist and adjust the lens of a camera to bring their subjects into focus, we too can view our God-given destiny with great precision and clarity. When properly dialed in, we can live our highest potential for maximum impact in the generation in which we live. The ultimate pleasure of our existence is found in our Creator's pleasure. That pleasure is felt when we are walking in the His perfect will. May the pages of this book help focus your lens to see with great detail the best life you were meant to live—one displaying, in full brilliance, His watermark.

CHAPTER ONE

Time Waits for No One

"Each of us is here for a brief sojourn; for what purpose he knows not, though he sometimes thinks he senses it. But without deeper reflection one knows from daily life that one exists for other people."

—ALBERT EINSTEIN[1]

EVERYTHING has a life span, a limited number of days. For example:

- According to the United States Federal Reserve, the average life span of a $100 bill is fifteen years, and a $5 bill lasts just 4.9 years.

- A car is considered an antique at twenty-five years old—if it can still operate that long.

- While a residential home may survive for hundreds of years, the individual components will not be as resilient. For example, a gas range, which has an average life span of about fifteen years, is one of the longest-lasting household appliances.[2]

People don't last long either. In North America, the average life span for men is seventy-seven years and eighty-one years for women. Life expectancy in Africa is the lowest of all continents at just sixty-one years and sixty-four years for males and females, respectively.[3]

With that sobering thought in mind, what are you going to do with your life?

With the few years we have each been afforded, how will you invest yours?

Because the human soul is eternal, its burning thirst for purpose and meaning can never be quenched by the temporal. But life has a way of duping us. Like an experienced con man, the daily grind of life does a bait and switch with things that don't really matter—a new car, a new house, a new outfit, a new relationship. But nothing stays "new" for long. We trade in cars, exchange homes for bigger and newer ones, and are constantly in search of something to satisfy. Material things carry with them an unwritten quality that no matter how fast, how shiny, or how many features they boast, it is never enough. Within us all, there is a dissatisfaction that begins to throb as soon as something newer comes along. In the end, the enticement of material things is simply a mirage and sends us on a path of searching that can never truly satisfy.

We then spend our most valuable commodity—time—upon things that only lead to delayed regrets. The correct question we need to be asking is not how will we *spend* our days here on earth, but rather how will we *invest* them?

Time will not stop while we wrestle with the correct answer. It will continue to plod along, all the while withdrawing from our account. I have often said to youngsters that they are rich and I am poor. When their puzzled expressions meet this statement I quickly explain, "You are rich in time, and I am growing poorer by the day." I quickly add, "Don't waste it."

Unearthing your destiny cannot be delayed. We were born into this generation by God's design to reach our highest potential. Time is our real enemy that must be overcome by redeeming it. Like a wild stallion, it must be tamed and brought under our control. It will wait for no one.

NOTES

1. Albert Einstein, *Living Philosophies* (New York: Simon & Schuster, 1931), 3.

2. Marcie Geffner, "What's the Life Span of a House?" Bankrate .com, January 22, 2010, https://www.bankrate.com/real-estate/ whats-the-life-span-of-a-house.

3. "Average Life Expectancy at Birth in 2018, by Continent and Gender (in years)," Statista.com, 2019, https://www.statista .com/statistics/270861/life-expectancy-by-continent.

CHAPTER TWO

Leaving What Is Comfortable

FULFILLING God's destiny and purpose will always require we leave what is comfortable. I have experienced this personally in my own life. When my wife and I left America to be missionaries in China, it required us to leave behind our jobs, our possessions, and everyone we knew. In so doing we received back the marvelous blessing of seeing many come to Christ who would have otherwise never heard about Jesus.

When our son was three months old, we left again for Czechoslovakia to live in a bus and preach on the streets. Communism had just fallen, and the nation was wide open to the Gospel. The journey required we leave what was comfortable, but we gained an amazing harvest of souls.

A few years later, we left a church we were leading to start an international student ministry called "Friends of Internationals." At that time, Lezli was eight months pregnant, and our son was five years old. Once again, we left behind what we loved, with only a promise from

God that He would bless us for our obedience. We experienced the great joy of seeing hundreds of students from all over the world come to Christ through that ministry, but it required we let go of the present.

Later, we moved again from Pensacola, Florida to Norfolk, Virginia to start Upward Church. As the church grew, we moved each time we planted one of our four current campuses. At present, we have seen hundreds of thousands of people come to Christ and millions more will in the future. In each case it required we let go of the present to inherit the future promise.

> *In each case it required we let go of the present to inherit the future promise.*

There is a journey of joy that God has planned for each of us if we are willing to leave our comfort zone and entirely pursue the vision God has given us. I believe there is so much more that God desires to do in all of our lives, if we are willing to pay the price.

The leaving that God requires is not always a geographical one. For some, God wants you to leave "just attending" a church and move into *serving* in it. Some need to leave the pain of the past and let go of bitterness, unforgiveness, and regrets. Some need to leave relationships that are holding you back. Some need to let go of a lifestyle that is above your means to allow you to be free to give and do what God wants you to do in the future. And we all need to leave the dinner table more often in order to fast and pray.

Before we were able to reach the numbers of people that we are now reaching, I wondered, *What does it take to make Jesus famous in the earth, and why doesn't God use me more?* I was so desperate to see millions of souls saved that I tried the most radical thing I could think of. I started doing forty-day fasts.

Please understand that I certainly believe that God honors any length of a fast; in fact, our church begins every year with a twenty-one-day church-wide Daniel fast. And please know that I am not telling you this to gain your esteem or admiration. I know that I am the little donkey that is carrying Jesus. But after much inner debate, I decided to write about this because I believe there is someone reading this as desperate as I was, and you will follow my example of fasting for souls. The cost of doing great things for God always requires we leave the comfortable behind, and that includes food.

I believe God is speaking right now to many of you as you read this. He is saying "My daughter, my son, there is so much more that I have for you." *"The plans I have for you,"* says the Lord. *"They are plans for good and not for disaster, to give you a future and a hope"* (Jer. 29:11 NLT).

Every good farmer knows that hard plowing always precedes the harvest. The Word instructs us to, *"Break up your fallow ground, for it is the time to seek the Lord, that he may come and rain righteousness upon you"* (Hos. 10:12 ESV). But our natural desire is to follow the path of least resistance. I can assure you that if you do follow the path of least resistance, you will fall far short of God's best for you.

You must start doing the last command you heard your Master give. The rest will not come until you start. Movement is the precursor to great things. It is much easier to turn the steering wheel on a moving car than one that is stopped. Good things happen when we are moving.

Risk is inherent in this journey. It must be present to reach your God-given destiny.

Risk is inherent in this journey. It must be present to reach your God-given destiny. That is what faith is: *"the substance of things hoped for, the evidence of things **not** seen"* (Heb. 11:1 KJV). God's plans always require risk. The best stories of great miracles are reserved for those who prevail against all odds, who climb mountains and scale rugged peaks. Will you live a great story, one that is worthy of telling? You will do so only if you live a life that is proactive rather than waiting for everything to come to you. To reach your full potential, to realize all the plans God has for you will require that you leave behind something or possibly someone.

CHAPTER THREE

No Place to the Devil

GOD is waiting to use us for greatness, but you and I have a real spiritual enemy who wants to thwart God's plan for our lives. It's important that we expose Satan's tactics that can keep us from fulfilling God's plan and purpose.

In Ephesians 4:27, Paul writes, *"Neither give place to the devil"* (KJV). The word "devil" comes from the Greek word *diabolos,* which is an old compound word that is made from the words *dia* and *ballo*. The first part of the word is the prefix *dia*, which means through, and often carries the idea of penetration. *Ballo* means to cast or to throw. These two words together mean the accuser, or to cast accusation.

The word "place" in this text is the Greek word *topos*. It refers to a specific, marked-off, geographical location. The word *topography*, as in topographical maps, is derived from this word. The Holy Spirit is saying through Paul—don't give the enemy any entry points from which to accuse you. Watch how you live. *"Be sober-minded; be watchful. Your adversary the devil prowls around like a roaring lion, seeking someone to devour"* (1 Pet. 5:8 ESV). Satan wants to penetrate our lives through any entry point that we allow. He wants to take it all, but he needs an entry point.

When we give place to the devil, our prayers are hindered. We don't come to God on solid footing. Those compromised areas in our lives allow the devil's accusations to stick. Unconfessed sin and unforgiveness are entry points that allow the devil to obstruct our prayers.

Did you know that even your marital relationship could be hindering your prayers?

> *In the same way, you husbands must give honor to your wives. Treat your wife with understanding as you live together. She may be weaker than you are, but she is your equal partner in God's gift of new life. Treat her as you should so your prayers will not be hindered* (1 Peter 3:7 NLT).

Your prayers are hampered when you don't treat your spouse properly. Some pastors can't understand why their prayers are not being answered. They think if they pray more, or harder, perhaps God will cause their churches to grow. In reality, they don't need to pray longer or harder; they simply need to get up, go home, apologize to their spouse, and make things right. They have given the devil access through their marriage and their prayers are hindered.

Some of the destruction that we encounter is of our own making. It is self-inflicted because we have given our enemy an entry point. The Greek in Ephesians 4:27 makes it clear that we choose whether or not to give the devil entry. You see, we have a choice in this. We can choose to "give the enemy place" in our minds and emotions, or we can choose not to have him there. We can shut every door, close every window, and seal every place in our lives through which the enemy would try to access us. We can prevent him from getting into the middle of our affairs! You and I never have to fall prey to the devil because, *"In all these things we are more than conquerors through him who loved us"* (Rom. 8:37).

When an entrance is not given, the enemy must vacate and leave. The scripture says, *"Submit yourselves, then, to God. Resist the devil, and he will flee from you"* (James 4:7). The Greek here means that Satan will run in terror away from you! I experienced the reality of this early in my ministry life.

A friend named Charlie Goddard was one of my first mentors. He was the first person to open the doors for me to preach in the County Juvenile Detention Center and in a soup kitchen he opened. One day, he approached me and said, "Hey, there is a self-proclaimed white witch who has come to the church, and she has asked for us to pray for her. She wants us to cast some evil spirits out of her. We are going to fast for three days, and then pray for her on Monday evening. We would like for you to come and help us."

Now, I don't know if this request is as shocking to you as it was to me the day he asked me, but I can tell you that this was not what I expected. Before I knew it, I blurted out, "Sure." There was no way I was going to let my mentor down. He was one of the first to see something in me that others didn't see. But after he left, I thought to myself, "What have I done?"

I drove home unable to fully comprehend that I had just agreed to cast the devil out of a white witch! As soon as I arrived home, I called my father, who was a pastor for thirty-plus years. When he answered the phone, I told him what I had just agreed to and asked him for his advice. He responded by saying, "Well son, if it were me, I would definitely watch and pray. I would pray with one eye closed and the other eye open!" His advice didn't give me a lot of comfort!

From that phone call I quickly decided that I needed to fast and pray with my other two friends on our newly formed prayer team. After three days we met together with the white witch. Before we started to pray, my mentor instructed me that because I was new to this I should just pray over in the corner. I was more than happy to oblige!

The two friends began to pray for the former witch as I stood in the corner and prayed. Over and over through the evening, they commanded whatever spirit they were dealing with at the time to come out. It was a full-on spiritual battle. The lady squirmed and spoke back to them in a deep demonic voice. The struggle went on for maybe thirty minutes as they worked to cast the first demon out of her. Finally, she coughed, screamed, and the demon came out. She collapsed to the floor, and peace enveloped her. You can tell from my eyewitness account that I took my father's advice; I watched and prayed!

During that evening, the same scene played out several times as different demons came out of the lady with brief periods of rest in between. As the evening wore on, the two praying for her became tired. That's when they ran into a very stubborn demon. They prayed and prayed, but this particular demon spoke in a devilish tone and boasted that he wasn't coming out. "You can't make me," it mocked.

When I heard his boast, I felt a wave of righteous anger come over me. Suddenly, I jumped up out of my corner and got right in the fray.

I told the lady to look at me, but the demon in her would not let her look me in the eyes. She kept moving her head away from my gaze. Then, before I could even think about it, I held her head and forced her to look at me. I commanded the evil spirit to come out of her in Jesus' name.

As she looked at me, the demon in her tried to intimidate me. Through her expression, it looked at me with pure hatred. Her face contorted, and her whole countenance changed. She growled at me like a dog and showed her teeth with her lips gnarled backward unnaturally. It was as if the demon was saying to me through her hellish expression, "You want me to look at you? OK, see how you like this!" Her eyes turned black, and the demon was actually snarling at me like a vicious dog through the poor lady's face.

For just a second or two I felt a pang of fear, but just as suddenly an amazing burst of boldness and authority washed over me. I looked that devil right in the eyes, and I shouted, "I said you *must* come out of this woman in the mighty name of Jesus!" She screamed at the top of her lungs and collapsed on the floor. The demon fled, and she was totally set free by the power of His blood. Hallelujah!

I believe in that moment as the demon glared at me that he was looking for an entry point within me. However, because we had fasted and prayed, there was none to be found. He had to flee. Again, the scripture says, *"Submit yourselves, then, to God. Resist the devil, and he will flee from you"* (James 4:7). A lot of people want to quote the last half of this verse while omitting the first part. But there is a condition that must be met before you can run the devil off. We must first submit ourselves to God, *then* we can command the devil to flee. If we want to be used mightily, to be a member of His special forces we must give no place to the devil in our life. But, friend, if you give the enemy a place in your life, this will not work for you. The sons of Sceva found this out the hard way. Here is their story:

> *And God was doing extraordinary miracles by the hands of Paul, so that even handkerchiefs or aprons that had touched his skin were carried away to the sick, and their diseases left them and the evil spirits came out of them. Then some of the itinerant Jewish exorcists undertook to invoke the name of the Lord Jesus over those who had evil spirits, saying, "I adjure you by the Jesus whom Paul proclaims." Seven sons of a Jewish high priest named Sceva were doing this. But the evil spirit answered them, "Jesus I know, and Paul I recognize, but who are you?" And the man in whom was the evil spirit leaped on them, mastered all of them and overpowered them, so that they fled out of that house naked and wounded. And this became known to all the residents of Ephesus, both Jews and Greeks. And fear fell upon them all, and the name of the Lord Jesus was extolled. Also many of those who were now believers came, confessing and divulging their practices. And a number of those who had practiced magic arts brought their books together and burned them in the sight of all. And they counted the value of them and found it came to fifty thousand pieces of silver. So the word of the Lord continued to increase and prevail mightily (Acts 19:11-20 ESV).*

The lesson here is, if you don't want to be running around naked and beaten, don't give the devil a place in your life! Don't go on the battlefield wounded. To have authority, you must be under God's authority.

> ## *If you don't want to be running around naked and beaten, don't give the devil a place in your life!*

To give no place to the devil requires that we protect the presence of God in our lives. We are told how to do this in the following passage:

> *Therefore be imitators of God, as beloved children. And walk in love, as Christ loved us and gave himself up for us, a fragrant offering and sacrifice to God. But sexual immorality and all impurity or covetousness must not even be named among you, as is proper among saints. Let there be no filthiness nor foolish talk nor crude joking, which are out of place, but instead let there be thanksgiving. For you may be sure of this, that everyone who is sexually immoral or impure, or who is covetous (that is, an idolater), has no inheritance in the kingdom of Christ and God. Let no one deceive you with empty words, for because of these things the wrath of God comes upon the sons of disobedience.*

Therefore do not become partners with them; for at one time you were darkness, but now you are light in the Lord. Walk as children of light…and try to discern what is pleasing to the Lord. Take no part in the unfruitful works of darkness, but instead expose them. For it is shameful even to speak of the things that they do in secret (Ephesians 5:1-8, 10-12 ESV).

The world places no value on His presence; in fact, the spirit of the world hates it, *"because their deeds are evil"* (John 3:19 BSB). They take His name in vain with no regret. They mock Him and persecute His children, and when you partake of the world and swim with the current, you lose His presence.

If we want God to work through us in great measure, we must be vigilant, always protecting the presence of God in our lives! David said:

I will ponder the way that is blameless. Oh, when will you come to me? I will walk with integrity of heart within my house; I will not set before my eyes anything that is worthless. I hate the work of those who fall away; it shall not cling to me. A perverse heart shall be far from me; I will know nothing of evil. Whoever slanders his neighbor secretly I will destroy. Whoever has a haughty look and an arrogant heart I will not endure. I will look with favor on the faithful in the land, that they may dwell with me; he who walks in the way that is blameless shall minister to me. No one who practices deceit shall dwell in my house; no one who utters lies shall continue before my eyes (Psalm 101:2-7 ESV).

David understood the value of protecting the presence of God in his life.

When we fill our minds with the right things, the devil finds no place in us. Ephesians 5:17-20 reveals how to live this way:

> *Don't act thoughtlessly, but understand what the Lord wants you to do. Don't be drunk with wine, because that will ruin your life. Instead, be filled with the Holy Spirit, singing psalms and hymns and spiritual songs among yourselves, and making music to the Lord in your hearts. And give thanks for everything to God the Father in the name of our Lord Jesus Christ* (NLT).

We are to be vigilant in renewing our minds; Romans 12:2 says *"but be transformed by the renewing of your mind."* Paul told the Philippian Christians to:

> *Fix your thoughts on what is true and good and right. Think about things that are pure and lovely, and dwell on the fine, good things in others. Think about all you can praise God for and be glad about* (Philippians 4:8 TLB).

The world is always trying to squeeze us into its mold, to be fashioned like it, and to be molded by it. That's what these translations of Romans 12:2 say: "Don't let the world around you squeeze you into its own mold. And do not fashion yourselves after this world." This scripture reminds me of farmers in Zentsuji, Japan. They grow watermelons for shipment—only they are no ordinary melons. They're square! They place them in tempered-glass cubes while they are growing and produce square watermelons. In the same way, the world continually tries to exert its influence on us as it attempts to shape us into its mold.

We are exhorted, "*Do not conform to the pattern of this world, but be transformed by the renewing of your mind*" (Rom. 12:2). When we allow the Word of God to work within us, it produces outward results, from the inside out. It does not permit external pressures to shape us.

The mind is the gate to how we respond and act, and you are its gatekeeper. What are you putting in your mind? Does your outward expression really represent your changed nature from within, or are you allowing yourselves to be molded and conformed to the world around you?

A beautiful illustration of how to protect the presence of God is found in the Old Testament tabernacle. The priests were commanded to keep the fire on the altar ever burning.

> *Command Aaron and his sons, saying, This is the law of the burnt offering. The burnt offering shall be on the hearth on the altar all night until the morning, and the fire of the altar shall be kept burning on it. ...Fire shall be kept burning on the altar continually; it shall not go out* (Leviticus 6:9, 13 ESV).

The fire first fell from heaven (see Lev. 9:24) and was maintained by the priests who constantly added fuel to it. What a beautiful Old Testament type and shadow of what should take place in Christ-followers today. We are to keep our lives on the altar and never let the fire from heaven go out! God has commanded us to come out of the world and be a distinct people.

> *For we are the temple of the living God. As God has said: "I will live with them and walk among them, and I will be their God, and they will be my people." Therefore, "Come out from them and be separate, says the Lord. Touch no unclean thing, and I will receive you." And, "I will be a Father to you, and you will be my sons and daughters, says the Lord Almighty (2 Corinthians 6:16-18).*

We are to be in the world, but not of the world (see John 17:14-16). Believers are to be insulated, not isolated, from the world. This truth is illustrated best by thinking of a submarine. Those vessels are fully functional in the water, but ruined if water comes within. If water gets into the submarine, there is cause to sound the alarm. But a submarine on the ground is also useless and is not able to accomplish its mission. Isolation from water is not the answer. The submarine must be in the water to function, and at the same time it must be insulated from the water. We are to be in the world but not of it. Even a trickle of the world left unattended can abort God's purposes in our lives.

You are the only one who can fill your mind with the right things. Nineteenth century author and minister J.C. Philpot wrote, "In proportion as we are conformed to the spirit of this world, our understanding becomes dull in the things of God, our affections cold and torpid, and our consciences less tender and sensitive."[1] Make no mistake, our lives are being changed either by pressure from without (conformation) or by His power from within (transformation). Romans 12:1 instructs us, *"I appeal to you therefore, brothers, by the mercies of God, to present your bodies as a living sacrifice, holy and acceptable to God, which is your spiritual worship"* (ESV). Our responsibility is to protect His presence in our lives. We are commanded to *"cleanse ourselves from all filthiness of flesh and spirit, perfecting holiness in the fear of God"* (2 Cor. 7:1 NKJV). We can do this because His grace enables us to do so.

Even a trickle of the world left unattended can abort God's purposes in our lives.

When our minds are renewed by the Word of God, we replicate the attitude of John the Baptist who declared, *"He must increase, but I must decrease"* (John 3:30). We take on the mind of Christ and become servants to others (see Phil. 2:5). We think less of ourselves by considering others more important than ourselves (see Phil. 2:3).

When we determine to give no place to the devil, God will even use our mistakes and our blunders for His purposes. I have often told people that I feel like my best plays for God have been my fumbles. In American football, I have watched offensive lineman, who never carry the football, try to pick up a fumble and run it into the end zone. Usually, when they attempt to do this, they drop it, then kick it, try to pick it up again, only to have it squirt out of their arms. Finally, in a last-ditch effort, they jump on the ball to gain possession of it for their team. The crowd then roars and stands to their feet in jubilation! The lineman stands up dazed and confused, only to realize then that he has jumped on the ball in the end zone. Touchdown! It is fumbled moments such as these that describe some of my greatest plays for God. Let me give you an example.

When I went to Pakistan, a great brother who was a former military EOD (explosive ordnance disposal technician) accompanied me. He felt strongly that he needed to go with me for my safety. I followed his precautionary recommendations to grow a beard and to color my hair and beard darker. The intention was to blend in with everyone else on our trip.

After our flight arrived in Pakistan, we followed all the fellow passengers to the customs line. We had just entered the line when two Pakistani border agents, dressed in military uniforms and armed with AK-47s, singled us out. They instructed us to follow them and bring all of our belongings with us. I saw other fellow passengers glance our way, trying very hard to be unobtrusive as they watched us being escorted away. At that point, I guessed that the beard wasn't working!

We followed the agents to a back room. It was cluttered with old records and file cabinets. We were instructed to sit down at a long, green wooden desk. A few more men in military uniforms entered the room, and then we were asked to surrender our passports. It was all very intimidating. The commander took our passports and then slid a questionnaire across his desk to each of us. We were to explain in detail why we had come to Pakistan. This caused our stress level to soar because we had already been singled out, and we both came to Pakistan on business visas that were arranged for us before our arrival. We could not say that we came to preach Jesus to 200,000 Muslims during Ramadan, but it was essential that our answers matched. We could not confer with each other because the agents were watching us intently. We knew that it was important that we appeared to be at ease as we both filled out our questionnaire.

That is when an incredibly tense moment turned into quite a wonderful experience. As I began to write down my answers, I was shocked to hear worship music playing softly over their speakers! It was great worship music too! Every ounce of trepidation and fear left as the worship lyrics brought peace to my soul.

I filled out the questionnaire with my heart full of gratitude to God, amazed that He was so good to go before us and prepare the way. I shook my head in amazement. Had our friends in Pakistan somehow arranged for the agents to pull us out of the line and play worship music to welcome us? I remember almost asking the agents if they were Christians, and then remembered where I was and thought better of it. I really couldn't make sense of it all, but the entire ordeal turned completely around.

We completed the questionnaires and gave them back to the agent with smiles on our faces. The worship music had worked! The agent applied an official seal to the back pages of our passports that read, "The Islamic Republic of Pakistan."

With passports and visas in hand, I looked over to smile in relief at my bodyguard Jason. It was at that moment that I noticed the blue light shining on my wireless headset. I put my headset in the outer pocket of my bag earlier when the flight landed. When we were escorted to the room, I placed the bag in the seat between us. What I didn't realize until that very moment was that as we sat down, I must have bumped my phone in my back pocket. When I did, the worship music I had listened to on the airplane started playing on my bluetooth headset. As it turned out, the awesome worship music that I thought was playing on their speakers was actually playing on my own headset!

My blunder changed what could have been a disaster into a touchdown! The worship music vaporized all the tension in the room. Just like the offensive lineman in the end zone, God used my mistake for a score! Touchdown!

> *It's not who we are that is important, it's Whom we carry that makes all the difference.*

Honestly, I can imagine that the whole time this was happening, Father God was laughing out loud in heaven. I think He was saying, "Craig, you are something else, but you are surrendered, so I'll use you."

If we will give no place to the devil, God will use even our mistakes and our blunders for His purposes. You may be the unlikely one or the one with colossal failures in your past, but just like Jonah and Samson, God will still use you greatly for His purposes.

It's not who we are that is important, it's Whom we carry that makes all the difference. What if the little donkey that carried Jesus into Jerusalem foolishly convinced himself that the loud praises that he heard were for him? What if he convinced himself that the palm branches placed in front of him were there because he was so special and the people didn't want him to hurt his little hooves? Poor little donkey, he didn't know Whom he was carrying! Don't be that donkey. Second Chronicles 16:9 says, *"For the eyes of the Lord run to and fro throughout the whole earth, to give strong support to those whose heart is blameless toward him"* (ESV). God is looking now for totally surrendered people who will give no place to the devil in their lives. As we are on mission, the joy of the Lord will be our strength.

NOTE

1. J.C. Philpot, "The Living Sacrifice," WiCWiki.org, accessed July 22, 2020, http://www.wicwiki.org.uk/mediawiki/index.php/The_Living_Sacrifice_Presented_2.

CHAPTER FOUR

Forward with No Fear

MY mind flooded with thoughts as I walked on stage. I looked out over the vast sea of dark-skinned faces and momentarily wondered what I had been thinking. It was Ramadan and I was a middle-aged white man standing before a crowd of over 200,000 Muslims getting ready to preach Jesus to them.

Before the crusade, I was fitted with a bulletproof vest that I was instructed to wear while preaching. However, when I put it on I felt the same sensation that David must have experienced when King Saul put his armor on the young shepherd boy to go face Goliath. Like young David, I knew I couldn't wear something that I had not tested. So I opted out of it and left it behind.

A security team escorted me to the crusade in a motorcade. The lead vehicle was a covered pickup with an armed security detail whose duty was to protect our driver and vehicle. The faces of the soldiers were completely covered except for their eyes as they openly brandished their weapons. The security team, both private and those provided by the government, were dressed in black. All were armed with AK-47 assault rifles. Behind us another security vehicle followed with more soldiers guarding our rear. The support vehicles stayed just in front of us and directly behind our SUV. Our caravan raced forward with sirens blaring and lights flashing toward the festival grounds. As we entered the grounds, the security team members fanned out and ran alongside our vehicle, weapons in hand. Three times *en route*, Muslim leaders warned us to shut down the meeting, but we kept moving forward.

When I arrived at the site, I was told that 179,000 people were officially counted within the stadium. But there were many more who stood on buses, in stairways, on buildings, and on the streets outside. The massive crowd formed a sea of people in all directions as they pressed toward the stage. The erected curtain walls around the event were bulging in from the crowd outside pushing closer to hear. Once inside, we were at the mercy of the crowd. An estimated 200,000 Muslims had gathered during the height of Ramadan in Pakistan to hear about Jesus.

As you read this, you may say to yourself, "Wow, this guy is brave!" Or perhaps you are saying, "Wow, this guy is an idiot!" I truly understand both of those responses! Allow me to explain that when we walk in total submission to God's will, we find that all fear is gone. It is not bravado or something we somehow muster up. When we fully commit to walk in our God-given destiny, we don't live in fear! There is no fear because Jesus Himself makes you brave.

Consider the apostle Paul's words found in Acts 20:23-25. In this passage of scripture, Paul was on his way to Jerusalem. He was walking in the known will of God for his life. He wrote:

> *I only know that in every city the Holy Spirit warns me that prison and hardships are facing me. However, I consider*

my life worth nothing to me; my only aim is to finish the race and complete the task the Lord Jesus has given me— the task of testifying to the good news of God's grace. Now I know that none of you among whom I have gone about preaching the kingdom will ever see me again.

Paul told his loved ones, "You will never see me again." His words were not for dramatic flair; he was speaking what he knew to be true by the Holy Spirit within him. He knew he was on a one-way trip!

Before I traveled to Pakistan, unlike Paul, I believed that I *would be* returning. Of course, we all knew the worst could happen. My wife and I sat down and went over all of our finances, and even delayed purchases, in case I didn't come home. I am the lead pastor of our church, so I spoke with our campus pastors and told them my wishes for the church if I did not return. I met with our financial board, and we settled on a contingency plan. That whole process made Paul's words even more incredible to me. Paul went to Jerusalem knowing he wasn't coming back. It is one thing to go on a missions trip believing you will return, but quite another to go knowing you will not. Paul knew by the Holy Spirit he would not return, yet nothing or no one could deter him. Under these extraordinary circumstances, Paul moved forward without fear.

The church I lead has physical campuses in military-base cities. As a result, our church family is filled with many military and special-force members. Trust me when I tell you that before going to Pakistan, they thoroughly briefed me of all the dangers. They made contingency plans, updated me on the current political climate, notified the State Department of my trip, and some told me I was crazy!

Yet, with all of their concerns, I kept moving forward because I knew God was calling me to go.

Like most of you, I have viewed recent articles of kidnapped foreigners and persecuted Christians kneeling moments before they are beheaded. I have seen videos of Christians burned in cages and the mass graves of those who died for their faith. Just one year prior to my trip, in the very city where I would travel, a video conference call I conducted with local pastors was postponed for forty-five minutes. It was delayed because those who were to attend couldn't get to the meeting place on time. The night before our call, twenty-six were killed in a bombing targeting Christians. The police blocked off the area and they were unable to get through. One year later, I traveled to that very place and sat in the very room where we our video conference meeting had taken place. I have written about this in great detail because it was in this crucible that God revealed a powerful truth to me.

Lord, make me brave whatever happens today. Please, Lord, don't let me ever deny Your name.

On the actual day of the crusade, I got up and prayed the same prayer that I had prayed for weeks, "Lord, make me brave whatever happens today. Please, Lord, don't let me ever deny Your name. If I am kidnapped, or worse, help me to stand strong."

As I prayed that prayer, I heard Him answer, "Why are you praying this?" He then gave these instructions: "I want you to remove yourself from this situation for a moment. Imagine it is someone else doing what you are doing. See yourself watching this person. That person has come to the Islamic Republic of Pakistan. They have come in the middle of Ramadan. They are going to preach a living Jesus to 200,000 Pakistanis in the middle of a Muslim city. If you were on the outside looking in at this person, wouldn't you call him brave?" Then He said this, "I've already completed what you are asking Me for, and I will make you brave for whatever I allow you to face in the future. You must only continue to walk in total obedience to My will, and then fear will never have a place in your life."

It was a stunning revelation. I was not brave because I had somehow mustered up all of my courage. In fact, it was nothing that I was even consciously aware of. He made me brave without me even knowing it! I was only focused on obeying what He had called me to do, and because of that surrender, fear was absent. Hallelujah!

Yes, fear will at times come like fiery darts to try to penetrate our peace, but in those moments we simply remind ourselves that we are walking in the known will of God for our lives. We can then move forward with confidence, knowing that whatever God allows will turn out for our ultimate good and for His Kingdom's advancement. It is this shield of faith that allows you to extinguish the fiery darts of the enemy!

If you are not living under Christ's Lordship, this kind of unwavering faith is not possible. Lasting peace is elusive to anyone who has not chosen total surrender to Christ.

Lasting peace is elusive to anyone who has not chosen total surrender to Christ.

Fear is on the rise. The Anxiety and Depression Association of America reported that "anxiety disorders are the most common mental illness in the United States, affecting 40 million adults in the United States age eighteen and older, or 18.1% of the population every year."[1] CNBC confirmed that "More than 40 million adults in the United States suffer from anxiety, and it is the most common mental illness in the United States. Overdose deaths involving benzodiazepines—such as Xanax, Librium, Valium, and Ativan, drugs commonly used to treat anxiety, phobias, panic attacks, seizures, and insomnia—have quadrupled between 2002 and 2015, according to the National Institute on Drug Abuse. The trend is being fueled by a 67 percent rise in prescriptions. The market for benzos, as they are called, is expected to reach $3.8 billion in the U.S. by 2020, reports Zion Market Research."[2] We live with as much plenty as we have ever known, yet many still live in fear.

Even many Christ-followers are afraid. They are afraid to share their faith. They worry they will not have enough in their retirement account, or they are scared they won't have what it takes to raise their children in this hostile environment. As the end becomes closer, fear will increase to greater levels. Jesus foretold. *"Men will faint from fear and anxiety over what is coming upon the earth"* (Luke 21:26 BSB).

Fear is present because love has not been perfected. God's Word emphatically states that, *"There is no fear in love. But perfect love drives out fear, because fear has to do with punishment. The one who fears is not made perfect in love"* (1 John 4:18).

In order for our love to be perfected, it requires total surrender to Christ's Lordship. That surrender enables you to walk in the known will of God for your life without fear.

The Book of Revelation is a sobering account of God's final judgment for all of mankind. In the middle of this book, we read what it takes to stand when everyone else is falling. While others receive the mark of the beast, curse God, hide in caves, and refuse to repent, a remnant will still stand in triumph. What will make this group different? The Bible says, *"They overcame by the blood of the Lamb, and by the word of their testimony. **They did not love their life, even to death**"* (Rev. 12:11 NHEB).

I have heard people actually quote this scripture and omit the last part. But it will take all three ingredients to overcome. I am quite possibly the world's worst cook; yet even I know that if you want the recipe to turn out right, you have to use all the required ingredients. To be an overcomer, all three of the ingredients given in the verse must be present in our lives.

It requires the blood of Jesus to cover our sins. The Bible says, *"without the shedding of blood there is no forgiveness of sins"* (Heb. 9:22 ESV). When John the Baptist saw Jesus coming into the water to be baptized, he exclaimed, *"Behold, the Lamb of God who takes away the sin of the world!"* (John 1:29 NASB). That blood will never lose its power!

Jesus came to earth to be the spotless, sinless substitute for your sins and mine. Without the cross, without His blood paying my debt and yours, we could never overcome. We have to acknowledge that

Jesus is either the world's worst liar or He is who He says He is—the only way to God. Jesus said, *"I am the way, and the truth, and the life; no one comes to the Father but through Me"* (John 14:6 NASB).

But this is not the only ingredient in the overcomer's recipe, is it? There are two more things needed. "The word of their testimony" is also mentioned. We must confess with our mouths that Jesus Christ is Lord (see Rom. 10:9). We have to say, like Peter, *"I am not ashamed of the gospel, because it is the power of God that brings salvation to everyone who believes"* (Rom. 1:16). Jesus said, *"Therefore everyone who confesses Me before men, I will also confess him before My Father who is in heaven"* (Matt. 10:32 NASB). We must speak up to be an overcomer.

The third ingredient is they did not love their life, even to death. This is when we begin to leave all to follow Jesus. We all know that talk can be cheap. If we are to be an overcomer, our walk must match our talk. This is total surrender. It is a surrender that compels us to push all of our chips on the table, a surrender that says, "Wherever You say to go, whatever You say to say, I will obey." It is an all-in approach.

I find that a lot of Christ-followers today want to double up on the first ingredient and leave out the last two. They are all about the blood of Jesus and a hyper-grace message, but they want to leave out the persecution that comes with confessing with their mouths that Jesus Christ is Lord. They are generous with the blood of Jesus because it costs them nothing. Jesus paid it all, but they don't want to take up their own cross to follow Him. They want nothing of this "loving their lives until death" talk. They are generous with grace but want nothing to do with the sacrifice it takes to truly follow Jesus.

In reality, they love this present world so much that their earthly life is the only one they are truly living for. It's easy to be generous with the blood of Jesus and live a sloppy life—all the while claiming grace. But Jesus Himself said, *"Whoever does not carry his own cross and come after Me cannot be My disciple"* (Luke 14:27 NASB).

Jesus declared this, so who are we to say different? He said it is not possible for us to be His disciples without bearing our own cross. An old hymn said it this way: "Must Jesus bear the cross alone, and all the world go free? No! There is a cross for everyone, and there is a cross for me."

The cross is an instrument of death, and as overcomers we must embrace it. Our attitude needs to be, "Whatever it takes." Paul said it this way, *"I die daily"* (1 Cor. 15:31 NASB). He said, *"I consider everything a loss because of the surpassing worth of knowing Christ Jesus my Lord"* (Phil. 3:8). Overcomers are willing to lay down their lives, even if it means death. Hebrews 11:13-16 says:

> *All these died in faith, without receiving the promises, but having seen them and having welcomed them from a distance, and having confessed that they were strangers and exiles on the earth. For those who say such things make it clear that they are seeking a country of their own. And indeed if they had been thinking of that country from which they went out, they would have had opportunity to return. But as it is, they desire a better country, that is, a heavenly one. Therefore God is not ashamed to be called their God; for He has prepared a city for them* (NASB).

So we much remember, it is only when all three ingredients—the blood of the Lamb, the word of our testimony, and not loving our lives unto death—are in the recipe that we can expect the right outcome.

The marvelous perk of being all in is that you begin to live without fear. Jesus makes you brave, whatever you face. It made Paul brave enough to move forward, even with the knowledge he would never return. The Bible says that the remnant in Hebrews 11:33-34:

> *By faith conquered kingdoms, performed acts of righteousness, obtained promises, shut the mouths of lions, quenched the power of fire, escaped the edge of the sword, from weakness were made strong, became mighty in war, put foreign armies to flight* (NASB).

They are the examples that we can face the future without fear! We can face the doctor's report without panic! I was empowered to preach in Pakistan without terror! Moving forward in the known will of God for your life enables us to confidently say, "My life is in His hands." Once that is settled, we can progress without fear, no matter what may come.

To move forward without fear, it is essential to know the steps that God has ordered for you to take before you move forward. Through prayer and fasting, God will reveal His plan for you. Jesus didn't say "if" you fast. He said, *"When you fast"* (Matt. 6:17). I am convinced that Christians see such little breakthrough because they don't fast. You see, fasting breaks the yoke! The prophet Isaiah wrote, *"Is this not the kind of fasting I have chosen: to loose the chains of injustice and untie the cords of the yoke, to set the oppressed free and break every yoke?"* (Isa. 58:6).

Fasting reveals the will of God and the timing of God. We need to know what to do and when to do it. The right results require the right action at the right time. The sons of Issachar, *"Understood the signs of the times and knew the best course for Israel to take"* (1 Chron. 12:32 NLT). Fasting gives us the same insight.

Fasting reveals the will of God and the timing of God.

We experienced this before my trip to Pakistan. I was scheduled to go one month before I actually went. Our church and intercessors were fasting, and several of them came to me, including my wife, and said, "We know you are supposed to go, but we feel very strongly the time is not now." At that point I had a choice to make—I could race through these caution lights or I could listen to godly counsel. Thankfully, I listened and made the hard choice of postponing my trip. Had I not listened to our prayer warriors, all the money, planning, and time necessary for a crusade of this magnitude would have been lost. Every flight into the country was shut down the week I was originally scheduled to be in Pakistan because India and Pakistan had a border skirmish. Fasting reveals God's will and timing to us.

This walk of faith I'm writing about is not in presumption or in denial of the circumstances and the dangers confronting you.

Progressing without fasting and prayer is presumption. Without prayer, you won't truly know His will for your life. You will move forward in the presumption that "God has got this." That kind of presumption can get you killed. There are many instances in scripture to support this.

An example of this kind of presumption is found in the story of Israel's journey into the promised land. The Book of Numbers records that Moses sent out twelve men to spy out the land and ten of these spies came back and gave a negative report.

> *So the men Moses had sent to explore the land, who returned and made the whole community grumble against him by spreading a bad report about it—these men who were responsible for spreading the bad report about the land were struck down and died of a plague before the Lord. Of the men who went to explore the land, only Joshua son of Nun and Caleb son of Jephunneh survived.*
>
> *When Moses reported this to all the Israelites, they mourned bitterly. Early the next morning they set out for the highest point in the hill country, saying, "Now we are ready to go up to the land the Lord promised. Surely we have sinned!"*
>
> *But Moses said, "Why are you disobeying the Lord's command? This will not succeed! Do not go up, because the Lord is not with you. You will be defeated by your enemies, for the Amalekites and the Canaanites will face you there. Because you have turned away from the Lord, he will not be with you and you will fall by the sword."*

Nevertheless, in their presumption they went up toward the highest point in the hill country, though neither Moses nor the ark of the Lord's covenant moved from the camp. Then the Amalekites and the Canaanites who lived in that hill country came down and attacked them and beat them down all the way to Hormah (Numbers 14:36-45).

Presumption will get you killed! Walking in the known will of God for your life is not a willy-nilly type journey. Presumption may lack fear, but it will get you in a world of trouble and may even cost you a premature death.

There is another example of presumption found in the Book of Joshua. God told Joshua and the Israelites to completely wipe out the inhabitants of their newly conquered land. They were to make no treaties with the locals, but the Israelites were deceived by the Hivites. These locals pretended to be something they were not.

The Israelites said to the Hivites, "But perhaps you live near us, so how can we make a treaty with you?" "We are your servants," they said to Joshua. But Joshua asked, "Who are you and where do you come from?" They answered: "Your servants have come from a very distant country because of the fame of the Lord your God. For we have heard reports of him: all that he did in Egypt, and all that he did to the two kings of the Amorites east of the Jordan.... And our elders and all those living in our country said to us, 'Take provisions for your journey; go and meet them and say to them, "We are your servants; make a treaty with us."' This bread of ours was warm when we packed it at home on the day we left to come to you. But now see how dry and moldy it is. And these wineskins that we filled were new, but see how cracked they are. And our clothes and sandals are worn out by the very long journey." The Israelites sampled their provisions but did not inquire of the Lord. Then Joshua made a treaty of peace with them to let them live, and the leaders of the assembly ratified it by oath" (Joshua 9:7-15).

But the truth of the matter was the Hivites actually lived nearby and resorted to deception so their lives would be spared. The Bible records:

But when the people of Gibeon heard what Joshua had done to Jericho and Ai, they resorted to deception to save themselves. They sent ambassadors to Joshua, loading their donkeys with weathered saddlebags and old, patched wineskins. They put on worn-out, patched sandals and ragged clothes. And the bread they took with them was dry and moldy. When they arrived at the camp of Israel at Gilgal, they told Joshua and the men of Israel, "We have come from a distant land to ask you to make a peace treaty with us" (Joshua 9:3-6 NLT).

The mistake the Israelites made was that they accepted things at face value. They sampled the bread and the wine. The Hivites' story seemed to check out. It looked right and sounded right, but they were deceived! The deception worked because the Israelites did not inquire of the Lord. They didn't go to God in prayer, and they moved forward in presumption.

It was through fasting and prayer that Jesus overcame the sin of presumption.

It was through fasting and prayer that Jesus overcame the sin of presumption. The temptation of Christ is described in the Gospels of Matthew, Mark, and Luke. According to scripture, after being baptized by John the Baptist, Jesus fasted for forty days and nights in the Judaean desert. During this time, Satan appeared to Jesus and tempted Him to sin. Jesus was tempted by the devil to act presumptuously.

> *Then the devil took him to the holy city and had him stand on the highest point of the temple. "If you are the Son of God," he said, "throw yourself down. For it is written: 'He will command his angels concerning you, and they will lift you up in their hands, so that you will not strike your foot against a stone.'" Jesus answered him, "It is also written: 'Do not put the Lord your God to the test'"* (Matthew 4:5-7).

Our Lord fasted and prayed to overcome the sin of presumption, so it's safe to say we need to as well. The absence of fear is not a life of presumption. It is not a life that presumes God will always cover you, even if your own laziness keeps you from fasting and praying to know His known will for your life. God doesn't cover impertinence.

We have a great enemy. The devil is a murderer, a thief, and a liar (see John 10:10). He plays for keeps. If we intend to go into his camp to plunder hell and populate heaven, we must prepare ourselves by fasting and prayer. If we want to walk in triumph, we must first "bind the strong man" (see Matt. 12:29). We must hear from heaven to know what to do and when to do it!

Moving forward in the known will of God is not presumption but neither is it denial. It is not an ostrich with his head in the sand approach. The Bible says that Abraham *considered his own body, which was as good as dead (since he was about a hundred years old)"* (Rom. 4:19 ESV). Abraham did not deny the fact that he was too old to have children. His faith was not a false faith that said we must never acknowledge or confess that there is an obstacle. Abraham acknowledged the problem, *"Yet he did not waver through unbelief regarding the promise of God, but was strengthened in his faith and gave glory to God"* (Rom. 4:20). Abraham was saying, "Houston we have a problem, but my God is bigger." A sure sign that we have faith in our faith, rather than faith in God, is that we cannot admit we have a problem to overcome.

A sure sign that we have faith in our faith, rather than faith in God, is that we cannot admit we have a problem to overcome.

Before I went to Pakistan, I set my house in order. I acknowledged that I might not return home. My faith was not damaged by that admission but was strengthened. My actions declared, "God, I trust You even in death, if that is what You allow, because I know You are telling me to go." It isn't rocket science. It's simply a matter of surrender. We pray as Jesus prayed: *"Yet not as I will, but as You will"* (Matt. 26:39 NASB).

Such surrender results in perfect love that casts out all fear (see 1 John 4:18). Fear's absence is not found in presumption or denial but only in a constant and total surrender. Christ perfects His love in us as we bow at His feet in total allegiance to our King. This surrender is described in the following verse:

> *Therefore, since we are surrounded by such a huge crowd of witnesses to the life of faith, let us strip off every weight that slows us down, especially the sin that so easily trips us up. And let us run with endurance the race God has set before us. We do this by keeping our eyes on Jesus, the champion who initiates and perfects our faith* (Hebrews 12:1-2 NLT).

Did you see in that last verse that Christ initiates and perfects our faith? We don't perfect our faith; Jesus does. You and I must simply surrender to the potter's hands. Most people readily recognize Jesus as the initiator of their faith, but most fail to understand that He is the perfecter of our faith (see Heb. 12:2).

How? Through the conflicts and trials that touch our lives. He perfects our love by stretching and challenging us through the difficulties of life. We often find ourselves questioning His love in the harshest of times, but in the midst of them His love is being perfected in us. If left to us, we would pick the easy path and travel from mountaintop to mountaintop, but Christ perfects our faith by leading us into *"the valley of the shadow of death"* (Ps. 23:4 NASB).

When we feel afraid, we need to go back to the altar of surrender and place the entirety of our lives on it again and again. This is a daily and continuous process that allows Christ to perfect His love in us.

If we will trust Him, even in the darkness when heaven is silent, His love will be so perfect in us that we can even face the Day of Judgment with *boldness! "By this, love is perfected with us, so that we may have confidence in the day of judgment; because as He is, so also are we in this world"* (1 John 4:17 NASB). We will be able to one day stand before a holy God and not be afraid. Wow! That is confidence!

When it comes to evangelism, we will never break the 10/40 Window without this fearless approach. We will only stand idly by and make excuses why it is impossible to accomplish. I love the words of the great missionary C.T. Studd who said, "Some wish to live within the sound of church and chapel bell; I want to run a rescue shop within a yard of hell."[3] That is the attitude required to plunder hell and populate heaven. No fear!

Living on mission repels fear. The life so many are searching for is only found when we are involved in the process of winning people to Christ. The absence of fear is found by those involved in the last task our Lord gave us to *go into all the world and preach the Gospel.*

NOTES

1. "Facts & Statistics," Anxiety and Depression Association of America (May 2019).

2. A. Garrison, "Antianxiety drugs—often more deadly the opioids—are fueling the next drug crisis in US," CNBC.com, (2018).

3. "20 Christian Quotes About Missions and the Great Commission," https://www.leadershipresources.org/blog/christian-quotes-about-missions.

CHAPTER FIVE

Faithfulness Is Required

THE lack of faithfulness is perhaps the most common reason why many people don't reach their full God-given destiny. One of the most common questions I am asked when people start hearing our story is, "How did you start doing this?" My first response is that it didn't happen overnight. My wife, Lezli, and I got our feet wet in ministry by going into nursing homes, a juvenile detention center, and a soup kitchen. We ministered in those venues during the week and preached one on one with people in the streets during the weekends.

In 1989 we quit our jobs, sold everything, and relocated to China to serve as missionaries. We lived there without internet, email, phones, hot water, and at times without electricity.

When communism fell in Europe, we moved to Czechoslovakia and lived in a converted public bus with our three-month-old son. We preached on the streets during the day and in a tent at night.

When we returned to America, we founded an international student ministry that spread to different college campuses. This ministry put us in the lives of students from all around the world.

Currently, I am the lead pastor of Upward Church, a multistate, multicampus online church with physical locations in Florida and Virginia. I travel back and forth between the campuses. Our media team streams the message live from my current location to all the other campuses each weekend. We have been in ministry now for over three decades. The mosaic of our lives has brought us to this monumental moment in mankind's history, "for such a time as this."

I run the risk of boring you with our story because I want to demonstrate that faithfulness is important. We didn't get to our current assignment overnight, and neither will you. Stay faithful in whatever God has given you to do right now. God still requires faithfulness. Jesus taught, *"Whoever is faithful in small matters will be faithful in large ones; whoever is dishonest in small matters will be dishonest in large ones"* (Luke 16:10 GNT). Faithfulness is key to maximizing your potential.

Faithfulness is key to maximizing your potential.

God wastes nothing in our lives. Just as Jesus had His disciples gather the leftovers when He multiplied the fish and loaves, He will redeem every act of our faithfulness. If we will stay faithful to our current assignment, one day we will look back and understand how the past has shaped our present. Let me give you an example.

We started Upward Church in Norfolk, Virginia with a leftover church group of about twenty-five people. Norfolk is home to the largest naval base in the world, and as a result Uncle Sam keeps moving people in and out of our area. Over the years, this ebb and flow has given us a network of beautiful Christ-followers for our global online campus. By necessity we learned how to do church at a distance, as we wanted to stay connected with our many deployed military families. Our online church leadership team is now located all over the world in places like Singapore, Japan, Spain, Africa, and many other distant places.

As our church grew, we ran out of room at our Norfolk campus. So, we planted other campuses. One of these opportunities was a fifteen-hour car ride away in Pensacola, Florida. A group of people from there had watched our services online and asked us if we would plant a campus in Pensacola. We agreed and my family and I moved to Pensacola to help start this campus. I now routinely fly back and forth between our campuses.

In the beginning, we pretaped Sunday morning's message during the week (with an audience of two cameramen) and replayed it on the weekend to the campus in which I was absent. This gave me years of experience preaching to thousands of people with no one in the room. My present was preparing me for my future.

After we planted the campus in Pensacola, we were given a church building and gymnasium in Williamsburg, Virginia. Once again, my family and I moved to plant a new campus. At one point we had five campuses in three different states, and I constantly traveled back and forth between them. The model was not sustainable, so we determined to find a better solution. That is when we started the process of acquiring software and media equipment to be able to consistently broadcast live from my location each week.

In addition to our weekend broadcast, each week we have multiple staff meetings through video calls. All of our weekly staff meetings are conducted this way. With so many miles between us, we had to be good at video conferencing. Technology is the key driver that enables our church model to work; we're able to bridge the distance gap and "do life together" from all around the world. The amazing thing is that our relationships have not faded in spite of the distance between us because we are together every week on the screen. Once again God was using our present to prepare us for our future. These experiences prepared us for the massive overseas video crusades we are doing now. God redeemed all of it, even the fragments, and He will do the same with your faithfulness. The tapestry of your life will all make sense one day!

> *The tapestry of your life will all make sense one day!*

Over the years, we have had guest pastors and entire church leadership teams join us to watch this process. As a result, we now have pastors as far away as Uganda in our weekly video calls. In these meetings, our screen is full of campus pastors, staff, and department heads who have joined us live for the meetings. This is our norm for doing church and has been for years, so when the opportunity came to use video technology to take the Gospel to the nations, we were well prepared. I wonder what God is using in your life right now to prepare you for your future?

Although live videos are our standard operating mode of doing ministry, a couple of things happened along the way that really highlighted its power. One event that really helped me to see the unlimited potential of building real community online happened between two of our own campus pastors. Every week we have all of our campus pastors on a minimum of two video calls. The first call is a campus-pastors-only call, and the second is our general staff call. At least once a year we all gather together at a central location for a planning meeting and schedule all of our message series for the next two years.

Several years ago, we had a new campus pastor at our Pensacola campus. He was with us for nearly ten months before our annual face-to-face meeting. I remember being on the flight with him, heading to our meeting in Atlanta, when he turned to me and said, "I really can't wait to finally meet Pastor Jesse (our Norfolk campus pastor) in person." I was so shocked! For months I had witnessed these two pastors interact with each other. By being on a video call twice a week with each other, they built a real and genuine relationship. These two were brothers in Christ. They were at a point in their relationship that they leaned on each other, prayed for one another, and could joke with one another. Their relationship with each other was so real and deep that I had forgotten that they had never personally met. That experience opened my eyes to the potential of building a real community by using video calls in small groups to bring people together from around the world. It was the next best thing to being in the very same room together, and where real community was possible. I had witnessed it in our two pastors, so I knew it could be done.

Converts are made in large meetings, but disciples are made in small groups. New believers have questions that need to be asked and answered. This cannot be facilitated in larger assemblies. To make disciples you must provide opportunities for people to get in real relationships with one another, to serve one another, and to be a part of a small group of people learning about Jesus together. Our wildly important goal for our online campus is to see people in real relationships with each other, in a real community. Seeing the relationship our two pastors enjoyed (a relationship that formed completely through video conferencing at the time) convinced me that a legitimate online church was possible.

Converts are made in large meetings, but disciples are made in small groups.

Somewhere in this time period, during a time of fasting, the Lord spoke to me and said, "From this point forward you will always speak to more people outside of the room than those who are in it." Then, He instructed me to lead our church in a major paradigm shift. He said, "Going forward, call your church an 'online church with physical locations' and never look back." Before we made that change, we were a physical church with an online presence. But once we began to function as an online church with physical locations, everything changed. Suddenly, there was a new commitment and obligation to build community online. We couldn't truthfully say that we were an online church with physical locations if we had no online campus staff, but we had multiple staff members for our physical locations. My first hire was my own daughter Candace who was finishing her last year of college at Liberty University.

As our online team developed, we realized that everything our physical campus provided, our online campus should aim to provide as well. Presently, our online campus has serving teams, prayer teams, small groups, and leadership meetings.

The second event that really showed me the power of video technology happened through a conversation I had with Candace after she had worked with our online campus leadership team for about a year. She made a startling comment to me over dinner one night. "Dad, this may sound weird, but I feel closer to our online church members than I even do with those in our physical locations." That was a "wow" moment for me. I knew how close she was to those at our physical location, so hearing this statement really revealed to me that real community was happening.

I know there is a lot of push back to online church attendance. There is the argument that it is always best to personally meet with others. That argument usually presupposes that those meeting online will never desire to gather with anyone else once they are in an online community, but I have found the opposite to be true. As people began to enjoy real relationships with others online, they naturally began to desire to gather together with others around them face to face. Many of our online campus members have started inviting others into their homes to do church together. Just this week, we had fifty-three people in attendance at one of our members' homes in Singapore. Instead of this military family on deployment existing all alone in a foreign country, the online campus has helped them form a community of believers in their home. This is not an isolated incident. We have seen it play out many times.

Today's generation interacts with their world through a screen. The screen is their translator, be it a smartphone, an iPad, or a LED screen. Many churches are stuck in the fifties. Some are busy fighting the very solutions needed to reach this generation. I believe many will be left with dying congregations and empty buildings that they can no longer afford to keep. If you want to fight that fight, that is your choice, but I think that churches that don't make a genuine effort to speak the language of the people (through screens) will resemble old Blockbuster stores in the next ten years.

It is sad that the church has historically been the last entity on the planet to embrace change, and only when they must change or die. I refuse to follow that path

It is sad that the church has historically been the last entity on the planet to embrace change, and only when they must change or die.

The third event that opened my eyes to the potential that video technology provides in reaching the entire world happened on a remote road in the middle of Africa. We were on a staff video call when we were joined by some of our pastors located in Uganda. They were returning from a video crusade we conducted that morning. They were bouncing around in their jeep through the bush of Africa at the same time video conferencing with our leaders who were scattered around the world. The signal was perfect! It was surreal. And to top it all off, the call was free. At that moment I realized that since we can conduct a video conference call in such a vastly remote area, with participants bouncing around in a jeep, we certainly could do this anywhere!

When we made the paradigm shift to become an online church with physical locations, suddenly our mission extended to the whole world. We are now equipped to fulfill our mission statement, "To reach as many people for Christ as fast as possible, and make disciples." We have stuck to this simple mission, and it is paying off now. There is no place out of our reach. Everything we do as a church, every dime we spend, goes through the filter of, "Will this help us to reach as many people for Christ as fast as possible, and make disciples?" This filter makes all of our staffing, outreach, and expenditure decisions so much easier. We always start with the "why," and that keeps us focused on the mission, and that mission is what fills us with joy.

I think it is important for you, the reader, to know that this next chapter detailing the journey we have been on as an online church was written and lived out long before the recent COVID-19 pandemic rocked our world. God went before us and positioned our church for this time. We are now able to lead other pastors and churches where we have already gone before. Let our story inspire you to be faithful in what God has presently called you to do. Only in hindsight can we fully appreciate all that God has done. Realizing our dreams require faithfulness.

CHAPTER SIX

Greater Is He

WE can move forward into our destinies without fear because the Greater One lives in us. Thirty years ago, my wife and I were teaching English at a university in China. We moved there just six weeks after the Tiananmen Square massacre. The country was under martial law, and we were at the same time leading many disillusioned students into a relationship with Jesus. Often harassed by the authorities, we met in secret, baptizing the new converts in our bathtub. It was harvest time in China, and we reaped from the work of many missionaries who planted seeds before us.

We only allowed thirteen believers at a time into our home. This was because everyone rode a bicycle to get there, and too many bicycles parked outside drew too much attention. We had back-to-back meetings several evenings each week because so many came to Christ who wanted to hear more and be discipled. To enter our meetings, they had to come at the set time and knock on the door a certain way. Once the meetings started, we played music loudly in the hallway while we met in our living room with the door shut and the curtains closed. Lezli would lead the worship. Each week she would have to constantly remind everyone not to sing too loud for fear that we would be heard.

Those were tense but glorious times. All of this was deemed illegal by the government, especially that we were engaging university students during that time of unrest. We were constantly aware of the need for caution as we couldn't risk anyone being caught in our gatherings.

Many of our Chinese students gave their heart to Jesus during the first semester of that school year. One student had the English name of Whitman, and he had a radical conversion. Whitman was on fire for God and was quick to share his faith. During the midyear school break on his train ride home, he shared with some people from his hometown that he was now a Christian. To his surprise they said they were too, and asked him if he would like to go to church with them.

"There are no churches or Christians in my town," he responded, to which they replied, "Oh yes, there are many. There are over 3,000 Christians there." Whitman was totally shocked, and praised God because he thought he was the only one!

They made arrangements so that on the next Sunday he was able to attend one of the many house churches in his hometown. Whitman was blown away by what he saw. Having lived there all of his life, he couldn't believe that right in his hometown was a house packed full of believers. He described how they stood on the beds, in all the rooms, and in the hallways just to hear their pastor.

After the message, the pastor asked Whitman to tell his church of what was happening in the universities. They had been praying for years for a move of God in the colleges, but had no means to monitor it. In those days, and largely it is still this way, the "peasants," as they were called, had no interaction with the "intellectuals" due to their very clear class system in place. Whitman informed them that God has sent many Christian English teachers to the universities who shared their faith and were leading many to Christ. He told them that this was how he came to faith. Upon hearing his report, the church broke out in spontaneous praise to God! Tears of joy flowed for the answer to their prayers.

As Whitman was about to leave, the pastor asked him to invite me to their house church meeting. They wanted me to come and share with them how God was moving in the universities. Whitman came back so excited, sure I would accompany him, but I knew the danger that I could potentially bring upon all of these precious believers. I sent him back to tell them that though I would love to meet them, I didn't want to put them at risk. I respectfully declined their request. But they would not have it. They said they knew the risk; they were at risk every day. They wanted to hear how God had answered their prayers and begged me to come.

Neither one of us knew my final destination in the countryside, but we had no fear.

The night before I was to go, my wife and I both felt such amazing peace. Neither one of us knew my final destination in the countryside, but we had no fear. I didn't go on presumption or without seeking the known will of God in the matter. We prayed, fasted, and consulted with another missionary couple we trusted and loved deeply. We were all in agreement that it seemed God was indeed calling me to go out to the countryside. So I moved forward without fear.

We hoped that I could attend this meeting without being seen, but that was not to be. I was about a foot taller than everyone else, very pale, plus I had on a bright red ski jacket (the only one we could find that fit me in China). On top of that, I didn't know it at the time, but I was going into a town that was off limits to foreigners. The communist government restricted access for foreigners so that they would not see the poverty of its people out in the countryside. So they banned them from certain areas.

When I stepped off the train platform, it became clear that most of the people in that town had never seen a white man before. I literally watched people crash their bicycles into each other as they stared at me. I was given the same reception that I imagine a Martian would receive!

Whitman and I made our way across town. He led me to an alley with hundreds of bicycles parked in tight rows. I could already hear the worship coming down the lane. It was bitterly cold and I shoved my hands deeper into my pockets as we walked the short distance. When we arrived at the apartment, the first person I saw was an elderly gentleman. The apartment was full, so he could not enter. So, he had taken off his hat and had his ear pressed to the glass window, to try to hear the praise and worship from within. There was literally no more room inside, so he stood outside in the snow and ice to participate in the meeting!

We pressed our way into the crowded apartment. Once inside, there were people standing everywhere. Every nook and cranny was packed. It was standing room only, except for two eight-foot long makeshift benches that each consisted of one two-by-four board supported by cement blocks. These boards were reserved for the elderly who could not stand. When Whitman and I entered, they insisted that we take a seat. We tried our best to decline, but they insisted. We were totally interrupting the meeting, so we sat down. The elderly people they moved, in order to give us a seat, could not physically stand. So, for the rest of that meeting, people took turns holding them up. There I was, squirming on my board after just thirty minutes, feeling so convicted when I looked around the room at these precious believers who had been standing for hours to worship Jesus—some of whom were now holding up others so I could have my seat. These people were hungry for God!

The pastor told everyone that the police had been there the week before. They had threatened the pastors and warned them that if they didn't stop holding the meetings, they would all be thrown into jail. The pastor then read the text where Jesus said, *"Do not be afraid of those who kill the body but cannot kill the soul. Rather, be afraid of the One who can destroy both soul and body in hell"* (Matt. 10:28). He said, "We are going to keep preaching Jesus to anyone who will hear us. We are ready to go to jail, and even give our lives should the Lord allow it. But we will not stop preaching Jesus."

It was the first time I heard someone say those words, and I knew he meant it. It galvanized something inside of me that day.

The pastor then asked me to preach because I was the missionary who had come all the way from America. I thought to myself,

"Who am I to speak to these people so committed to the Kingdom?" I said, "Please no, Pastor, I need to learn from you." But again, they all insisted. As I humbly stood and shared with them what God was doing in the universities, they wept tears of joy.

While there, I gave all of the pastors a reference Bible in their own language. They had never seen one before that day. As they received their Bibles, I saw every emotion known to man sweep through them as they held their new treasure close. They cried tears of joy one moment and then laughed the next. It was one of the most rewarding moments of my entire life.

We shared a meal afterward, and then it was time for me to make my way back home. I was so moved by that experience that I wanted all of our new believers to travel to this church to see their own people worshiping God openly and without fear.

We couldn't send too many at one time without drawing attention, so the next week we sent a handful of students to the underground church. They had quite a shock when they arrived. All of the Christians were still meeting, but they were listening to a cassette tape of the prior week's message. The pastors had been thrown in jail.

The pastors had been thrown in jail.

The next Monday, the police found Whitman and told him that if I didn't give myself up willingly, they would come to arrest me. A few days later, I took the same steam-driven train ride deep into the countryside and turned myself in. When I arrived, I learned that the pastors had spent a week in jail before their release. I also learned that I had broken five Chinese laws: I came to an off-limits town, gave out unregistered Bibles, gave the church an offering, preached to Chinese nationals, and preached at an unregistered church meeting. They were all good laws to break! However, I was caught red-handed. The police had an underground policeman planted in the meeting I took part in. The spy was sent to see if the local pastors would defy their warning, and as an extra bonus, I showed up!

When Whitman and I arrived at the police station, we were escorted past dirty cells full of hopeless looking men. They did this to intimidate us. Then we were taken into a room that looked like it was from an old Humphrey Bogart movie. There was one green table and chair in the center of the room. A single light bulb hung over the wooden desk, with one policeman on the other side of the desk and another mugging at us from the corner. He sat in the shadows and never spoke a word. For the next several hours, my interpreter and I were interrogated. We were asked the same questions over and over again. They wanted to know what business we had there. We gave the same answers repeatedly until finally, the lead interrogator said to me, "We believe that you are a spy sent to our country. You say that you are a Christian. Can you prove it?"

It was at that very moment that the Holy Spirit spoke to me and said, "This is why you've been brought here. I want you to share your testimony with this man." That one word from God changed everything for me. I went back to the very beginning of my life with Christ. I shared everything that I could possibly remember that God had done for me. As I did, my fear began to turn into God-given confidence. The Holy Spirit began to flood into that locked room and He filled it. There, in that remote area of China, in the interrogation room of that police station, God showed up on my behalf.

There, in that remote area of China, in the interrogation room of that police station, God showed up on my behalf.

By the end of my testimony, I felt such peace, such an overwhelming sense of God's presence, that I said with boldness to the officer, "Sir, God loves you so much, He not only sent His Son Jesus to die on a cross for your sins, but He has sent me halfway around the world to tell you this story. You don't have to die in your sins. Jesus took our place and paid the debt we could never pay. You can be forgiven and receive God's marvelous grace right now. No matter how low you think you've gone, God's grace is deeper still."

He was sitting with his feet on the desk, and when I concluded with, "God's grace is deeper still," it was as if someone punched him in the gut. His feet came flying off the desk, and he rolled back in his chair. He let out a loud grunt, and then said through the interpreter, "I'll hear no more of this! You are free to go. Get out of my station!"

I was so sad to see him resist the Holy Spirit, but I was glad the interrogation was over. I walked out of that jail a free man, knowing that God sent His Spirit to set us free. Not one American was aware of where I was located. My own wife didn't know where they took me. So, if I had been locked in that jail, I don't know that I would have ever come out, but God set me free!

As we turned to leave the jail, we were once again escorted past the cells where the stares of the hopeless inmates confined there followed us. The reality of how Christ set me free from this physical prison, and from the prison of sin that once held me captive, was overwhelming. I don't think I walked out of that prison; I floated! I tell you, *"Greater is He who is in you than he who is in the world"* (1 John 4:4 NASB).

Thirty years later, I felt the same peace and boldness while in Pakistan. The morning of the massive crusade, I woke early to have my quiet time with the Lord. In prayer I was taken to Psalm 91:4-5 and Psalm 46:8-11. Those verses took on such new meaning as I read them that morning. I preached to 200,000 Muslim people, during Ramadan, without a bulletproof vest, but I had something better. Psalm 91:4-5 says, *"He will cover you with his pinions, and under his wings you will find refuge; his faithfulness is a shield and buckler. You will not fear the terror of the night, nor the arrow that flies by day"* (ESV). This verse says our God is better than a flak jacket! It says that no projectile aimed against you shall harm you. His faithfulness shall be "your shield and buckler." What a promise to receive from the Lord on the very day I needed it!

Our God is better than a flak jacket!

Then He took me to this promise: *"He makes wars cease to the end of the earth; he breaks the bow and shatters the spear; he burns the chariots with fire. 'Be still, and know that I am God. I will be exalted among the nations, I will be exalted in the earth!' The Lord of hosts is with us; the God of Jacob is our fortress"* (Ps. 46:9-11 ESV). God's Word says that "He breaks the bow, He shatters the spear"—these are all projectiles that God declares useless. No bullet, no suicide bomber, and no weapon of any kind will prosper! He says, "I Myself am your fortress!" He is greater than any threat! I preached that night with total peace.

The Greater One has protected me all through my life. Once, I led a mission team to Tanzania to do a crusade. On the flight home, our plane stopped to refuel in Nigeria. We were told to disembark the plane while they refueled. When the time came to reboard our aircraft, the ticket agent claimed that one of our team members did not have a ticket. He said the rest of us were free to embark, but he would not be able to board. We tried to reason with the agent that we had all been on the plane together, and just disembarked as instructed. But he refused to budge. He told us to move aside until he called us. That's when an American couple who was stranded there came over to me and whispered, "Don't go over to the side and sit down until he calls you back up to the counter. He did the same thing to us last week. We have been stranded here since. We have learned that the agents are reselling sold seats to the locals at a discounted price. We have been stuck here a week, without visas for this country."

When this couple told me their story, I immediately knew where the real fight needed to occur. This verse says, *"For our struggle is not against flesh and blood, but against the rulers, against the authorities, against the powers of this dark world and against the spiritual forces of evil in the heavenly realms"* (Eph. 6:12). As I began to take authority over the devil, my eyes caught the agent's nametag for the first time. His English name was Snake.

I told the rest of the team to get on the plane and start praying. Mr. Snake continually told us to step aside, but I would not yield. I stood at the ticket counter praying silently and steadily moving my teammate's old boarding pass to the top of the pile of tickets. They repeatedly warned me that if I didn't board, I would lose my seat as well. I did not budge. Mr. Snake then called for the airport security, but I held my ground. When the security members came, I pleaded our case with them, but no one would listen. It looked impossible, but the whole team was praying. Finally, I looked Mr. Snake right in the eyes and I said, "This plane is not leaving without us; we are getting on this plane in Jesus' name!" I felt heaven's authority behind my words, and just like that the battle was over. After forty minutes of intense spiritual warfare, they just gave up, handed us a boarding pass, and we got on the airplane. The Greater One was our defender, and He made a way where there was none.

If we are to live the great adventure God has planned for all of us, we must settle within our hearts that the Greater One fights for us. Yes, we are fighting raw evil and gross spiritual darkness, but Jesus has given us His authority over the enemy of our souls. All of heaven's host backs us up. We have no reason to fear, for the Greater One lives in us! When God asks us to do something there is always a measure of fear attached to it. This fear tries to immobilize us. Fear comes from the uncertainty of not knowing how things will turn out prior to our leap of faith. If we allow fear to dominate our lives, we will never walk in our God-given destiny. Take the plunge, trust God, for He is more than able to make you succeed. No fear!

CHAPTER SEVEN

You Are Qualified

I want to assure you that you are qualified to be a part of this mission. Even if you feel you are the most unlikely or unqualified person, you should know that God historically picks the unlikely and unqualified. If you have failed in epic fashion, you are a perfect candidate because God chooses the unlikely and the failures.

If there was ever a "golden boy" in scripture, it was Samson. He was one of only three divinely announced births. Before Samson's birth, God called him to be "set apart" for His purposes. He had great parents, was handsome and strong, and obviously had God's favor all over him.

If anyone should have gotten it right, it was Samson. But Samson struggled with lust and got into trouble with women repeatedly. His fall was epic and well documented. *"Then the Philistines took him and put out his eyes, and brought him down to Gaza. They bound him with bronze fetters, and he became a grinder in the prison"* (Judg. 16:21 NKJV).

Delilah woke Samson from sleeping on her lap when his failure and her betrayal were complete. Samson's story contains some of the saddest and most sobering words found in the Bible: *"So he awoke from his sleep, and said, 'I will go out as before, at other times, and shake myself free!' But he did not know that the Lord had departed from him"* (Judg. 16:20 NKJV).

Like Samson, those who habitually continue in their sin wake up one day and don't realize that the Lord has departed from them. There are many people today who, like Samson, have repeatedly spurned the Holy Spirit's instruction to live a godly life. The Bible tells us that it is God's grace that teaches us to live a holy life, *"For the grace of God that brings salvation has appeared to all men, teaching us that, denying ungodliness and worldly lusts, we should live soberly, righteously, and godly in the present age"* (Tit. 2:11-12 NKJV).

The grace that brings us salvation is not a license to sin but a teacher against it. Those who repeatedly spurn the Holy Spirit's voice sear their conscience. Their willful sin insults the Spirit of grace and brings with it an expectation of judgment.

The grace that brings us salvation is not a license to sin but a teacher against it.

For if we sin willfully after we have received the knowledge of the truth, there no longer remains a sacrifice for sins, but a certain fearful expectation of judgment, and fiery indignation which will devour the adversaries. Anyone who has rejected Moses' law dies without mercy on the testimony of two or three witnesses. Of how much worse punishment, do you suppose, will he be thought worthy who has trampled the Son of God underfoot, counted the blood of the covenant by which he was sanctified a common thing, and insulted the Spirit of grace? (Hebrews 10:26-29 NKJV)

We can reject the path that Samson took and gain much by learning from his mistakes. His story is recorded and written for our benefit so that we don't take the same path. Let's take a closer look. The following passage details the events that led to his failure:

And it came to pass, when she pestered him daily with her words and pressed him, so that his soul was vexed to death, that he told her all his heart, and said to her, "No razor has ever come upon my head, for I have been a Nazirite to God from my mother's womb. If I am shaven, then my strength will leave me, and I shall become weak, and be like any other man." When Delilah saw that he had told her all his heart, she sent and called for the lords of the Philistines, saying, "Come up once more, for he has told me all his heart." So the lords of the Philistines came up to her and brought the money in their hand. Then she lulled him to sleep on her knees, and called for a man and had him shave off the seven locks of his head. Then she began to torment him, and his strength left him (Judges 16:16-19 NKJV).

Samson played with sin and was burned. Unlike Joseph, who ran from Potiphar's wife and her sexual advances, Samson kept getting closer and closer until he revealed the secret of his strength to Delilah. This passage tells us, *"she pestered him daily with her words and pressed him, so that his soul was vexed to death"* (Judg. 16:16). Samson didn't distance himself from temptation; instead, he stayed in close proximity to it. When we flirt with sin and choose to live in the gray areas of life, eventually we will get burned. Scripture asks the question, *"Can a man take fire to his bosom, and his clothes not be burned?"* (Prov. 6:27 NKJV).

> ## When we flirt with sin and choose to live in the gray areas of life, eventually we will get burned.

When Samson was lulled to sleep on Delilah's lap, it was a prophetic image of what sin does to us. Unconfessed sin will put us to sleep spiritually. Our conscience then becomes dull and insensitive. We naïvely press on, unaware of the great price we will pay. Willful sin will always cost us more than we wanted to pay, keep us longer than we wanted to stay, and take us further than we wanted to stray. When we consistently compromise what is right, we lose the ability to stay alert to the enemy's tactics and thereby allow him to wreak havoc in our lives. The Bible warns us to, *"Be sober, be vigilant; because your adversary the devil walks about like a roaring lion, seeking whom he may devour"* (1 Pet. 5:8 NKJV).

Samson violated every warning that God sent his way. In the end, it cost him his eyesight and his freedom. There is a message in that to us. All who choose to continue to go their own way, after the Lord has repeatedly warned them to repent, will lose their spiritual eyesight and eventually will be held totally captive to their sin. Those who reach that point become so self-deceived that they justify their sin and become angry with anyone who dares to challenge them.

Have you met someone like that? They always explain why the Bible doesn't really mean what it says about their sin. They spin the scripture to mean something else entirely. Their spiritual eyes have been gouged out, and they don't realize that the Lord has left them.

When we fail God, it becomes easy for us to listen to the voice of the enemy as he shouts in our ears, "You're not good enough. You've blown it so badly that God will never use you again. You're just a big hypocrite." But God is the God of second chances if we will just repent and change directions!

Samson chose his own way, and in doing so lost everything dear to him before he called upon the Lord one last time.

> *"O Lord God, remember me, I pray! Strengthen me, I pray, just this once, O God, that I may with one blow take vengeance on the Philistines for my two eyes!" And Samson took hold of the two middle pillars which supported the temple, and he braced himself against them, one on his right and the other on his left. Then Samson said, "Let me die with the Philistines!" And he pushed with all his might, and the temple fell on the lords and all the people who were*

in it. So the dead that he killed at his death were more than
he had killed in his life (Judges 16:28-30 NKJV).

Due to all of his failures, most people would have given up on Samson. As he stood by those pillars, with his eyes plucked out and bound in chains, most would have given him little chance that God would use him again. It's easy to think because he had so much advantage, only to squander it, that God would be done with him. But Samson asked the Lord for one more chance to make a difference with his life, and God responded!

God will do the same for *anyone* who will abandon their sin and ask Him for a second chance. We see repeatedly in the Bible how God often uses for His purpose those who have failed in the past. In fact, Samson's greatest victory came after all of his many failures.

> *God will do the same for anyone who will abandon their sin and ask Him for a second chance.*

Jonah took the same path that Samson traveled. He deliberately disobeyed the Lord's instructions and even chose the opposite direction of where God wanted him to go. Jonah's documented journey is telling. The Bible records for us that Jonah fled from the presence of the Lord and went down to Joppa, down into the ship, down into the lowest part of the ship, laid down, and fell down into unconsciousness. He was fast asleep. (Sounds like Samson, doesn't it?) He was thrown down into the sea and swallowed down into the belly of the great fish. By now we should all understand that the path away from God and His calling for our lives is a downward spiral.

Jonah's story should also teach us to never write off the prodigals in our lives. It may appear that they will never come back to God, that they are too far gone, but don't ever give up hope. Jonah was so stubborn, so set on doing his own thing that it took three miserable days in the belly of a great fish before he came to his senses!

Jonah's story parallels the story of the prodigal son:

> *Not long after that, the younger son got together all he had, set off for a distant country and there squandered his wealth in wild living. After he had spent everything, there was a severe famine in that whole country, and he began to be in need. So he went and hired himself out to a citizen of that country, who sent him to his fields to feed pigs. He longed to fill his stomach with the pods that the pigs were eating, but no one gave him anything* (Luke 15:13-16).

Like Jonah, this prodigal had gone as far down as a young Jewish heir could possibly go as he took care of someone else's pigs—which are unclean animals to the Jewish people. He had gone down away from his father's presence, spent his account down to nothing, stooped down from an heir to a servant, was down in the pigpen, and was so hungry that he wanted to eat the pig's slop. Again, we see that the path away from God's presence is always down. Without repentance, it ultimately leads all the way down into hell itself.

Thankfully, the prodigal son, Samson, and Jonah each finally came to their senses and changed their direction. The prodigal returned home and begged for forgiveness, Samson cried out to God and was used by the Lord one last time, and Jonah finally came to his senses in the belly of the great fish. From inside the fish, Jonah prayed to the Lord his God. He said:

> "In my distress I called to the Lord, and he answered me. From deep in the realm of the dead I called for help, and you listened to my cry. You hurled me into the depths, into the very heart of the seas, and the currents swirled about me; all your waves and breakers swept over me. I said, 'I have been banished from your sight; yet I will look again toward your holy temple.' The engulfing waters threatened me, the deep surrounded me; seaweed was wrapped around my head. To the roots of the mountains I sank down; the earth beneath barred me in forever. But you, Lord my God, brought my life up from the pit. When my life was ebbing away, I remembered you, Lord, and my prayer rose to you, to your holy temple. Those who cling to worthless idols turn away from God's love for them. But I, with shouts of grateful praise, will sacrifice to you. What I have vowed I will make good. I will say, 'Salvation comes from the Lord.'" And the Lord commanded the fish, and it vomited Jonah onto dry land (Jonah 2:1-10).

Many of us know how his story ends. God used Jonah to turn an entire city in repentance. We know that God used Jonah in an incredible way, but before we race to the end of Jonah's story, I think there is a great benefit in taking a longer look at Jonah's life immediately after the fish vomited him up on the seashore. Here we find a guy with seaweed wrapped around his head. He stinks and he looks worse than anything we have ever witnessed. Imagine Jonah on that beach drenched in fish vomit and coated in sand. In that moment, who would look at Jonah and say, "I see a great man of God"? In his sorry condition, who would believe that one day God would use this man as a great evangelist to turn around an entire city? And if we knew that Jonah arrived in this state because he purposely disobeyed and ran from God's will for his life, who would have given Jonah any chance that God would use him again in any measure? But God chooses the unlikely and the failures. When we see Jonah on that beach, it should remind us that God is the God of second, third, and infinite chances. Jonah was down to his final prayer when the last-minute God granted him a second chance. Our Jesus is the great Redeemer! His grace cannot be comprehended.

With this backdrop, let me tell you a story of modern-day redemption likened unto Samson and Jonah's story. This is a story of a mother who failed God miserably, and yet God gave her a second chance.

At one of our video crusades in Uganda, a very connected witch doctor came to know Christ. After her conversion she then helped us to rescue children who were to be murdered and offered to demons as human sacrifices. We then housed and fed those children for months until they could be placed in homes. I know that it is very hard for us in the West to even imagine such horrors, but the gross spiritual darkness is so thick in these remote areas that parents often succumb to the demonic activity and lies of witch doctors for fear of their own lives. They are told they will all die if they don't give up one of their babies.

We learned of one mother who was so overcome with guilt and shame after she surrendered her son to the witch doctors that she fled from that area where she lived. This happened before our video crusade was held in her city. The mother stayed away for months, until she was finally forced to return home. Filled with condemnation and remorse, she decided to go to the newly established local church we started in her hometown. She wanted to ask Jesus if He could possibly forgive her and give her a second chance. She hoped she could somehow come out from under the avalanche of guilt she felt for her actions.

What happened next was absolutely marvelous. When this mother came to the church to find Jesus, she also found her son— alive! She did not know that while she was away, we rescued her son with thirty-one other children the night before they were scheduled to die. He was one of the children we fed and clothed for months at the orphanage. The entire church erupted in praise to God as they watched the tearful reunion of mother and son.

Your failures do not disqualify you.

Anytime you think you are past redemption, remember this mother who gave up her son to be a human sacrifice. She received a second chance, and so can you. No matter how far you've fallen, no matter how unlikely you feel you may be, God is just waiting for you to ask Him for another chance. Your failures do not disqualify you. God has a grand plan to use you in great measure.

CHAPTER EIGHT

This Generation's Opportunity

HOW far could technology take you toward your God-given destiny if you leveraged it properly? Today's technology enabled our ministry to witness nearly 800,000 decisions for Christ in just twenty months. What is even more incredible is that I believe that other churches and individuals can repeat what we have accomplished and surpass it. When we embraced the tools available to us today, we found ourselves in places we never thought we would go.

The tools of this generation granted me access into the 10/40 Window. This window contains 97 percent of the unreached people in the world, with only 10 percent of the missionary force working there. In many of these nations Christians are persecuted and killed. Many of these governments oppress the church and oppose the Gospel. It all sounds very bleak until we realize that new video technology allows us to take the Gospel to places that were once out of our reach.

Our generation has a new reality. The unreached nations of the earth are no longer waiting on God; *they are waiting on us*. God has given our generation the tools we need to reach them.

> ## *The unreached nations of the earth are no longer waiting on God; they are waiting on us.*

Here is my point—if God can accomplish this through us, what could your life look like if you discovered God's will for your life and embraced the generation into which you are born? How can you leverage technology to reach your highest potential?

What would you say if I told you that in one week, I preached to three continents, six nations, won 100,000 people to the Lord, and then drove to my hometown Starbucks and had my favorite cup of coffee each afternoon of those outreaches? I didn't have to buy an airplane ticket, bring my passport, or get a visa for those crusades. I just used my computer. And it has continued:

- In just three nights of 2019, a total of 311,987 people came to Christ in the Islamic Republic of Pakistan.

- One night in March, 81,554 people confessed Jesus as their Lord.

- With April came another 77,184 new Christ-followers, and as a result, 21,536 cell groups and 7,000 home churches were formed.

- One glorious night in May, 153,249 people in Pakistan gave their lives to Jesus in a single meeting.

These outcomes were entirely impossible in any earlier era. Today's technology opened doors held shut for generations. Those who came to Christ were all in the 10/40 Window. This was their first time to hear the Gospel. The tools of a new generation made this possible. We worked outside of the box and did something that had never been done before.

To get some perspective on the possibilities of our times, let's examine a little church history. When Peter stood up and preached on the Day of Pentecost, three thousand people were added to their number. The largest crowd that Jesus spoke to was, *"about five thousand men, besides women and children"* (Matt. 14:21). According to Billy Graham's website, the largest number of salvations recorded on a single crusade night was 75,000 people.[1] In a five-year period, during the Brownsville Revival, a "reported 200,000 people gave their lives to Jesus Christ."[2] But this year, in just three nights during our crusades, 311,987 people came to Jesus in just one of the nations where He is moving! An end-time harvest is being gathered right now and in a surprisingly new way.

God is working through modern technology in an unprecedented manner. In the March crusade just alluded to, several large LED screens were put in place for a crowd of 92,261 people. Just before the crowd arrived, it began to rain. The owner of the rented LED screens told our team that he would need to dismantle them due to the weather. But, knowing that eternity was at stake for thousands of people, the local pastors and intercessors gathered in a circle and cried out to God for the rain to stop. As their prayers rose to heaven, the clouds parted, and a clear sky appeared! The equipment owner was so moved that he left the screens in place. Not another drop of rain fell that night, and 81,554 Pakistanis came to the saving knowledge of Jesus Christ!

As their prayers rose to heaven, the clouds parted, and a clear sky appeared!

What may surprise you further is that the main speaker was not present at the event. The sermon the crowd heard, and the preacher they saw, was on a video screen. I spoke to that vast crowd in Pakistan from my home church in Pensacola, Florida. I didn't need a visa or an expensive airline ticket because it was all done from my hometown. Our God is fulfilling His promise that His Word will never return void, even if it is being transmitted by satellite from one side of the world to the other!

I have often joked when sharing these testimonies that the apostle Paul must be rolling over in his grave. He is saying, "It's not fair! I was shipwrecked, bitten by a snake, stoned and left for dead, beaten with rods, and went through countless hardships. Now, this generation is preaching the Gospel to thousands of people all around the world in the morning and having a cup of Joe at their favorite coffee shop in the afternoon!" It must seem so very unfair to those who have gone before us.

Missionaries of old purchased one-way tickets to faraway lands, knowing that they would never return home. Yet in our day, we can now preach to massive crowds on various contents and nations to see hundreds of thousands of people saved without ever leaving our hometowns.

The apostle Paul, and even Jesus himself, didn't have the means of communication we currently possess. But now, our generation can finally complete the last task Jesus gave His followers to, *"Go into all the world and preach the Gospel to all creation"* (Mark 16:15). We now have the modern video technology needed to finish the job! No other generation has had this opportunity. If we don't use it to advance His Kingdom, how will we be able to answer for that? What excuse would stand before a God who was willing to give His one and only Son so all could be saved?

As I stated earlier, we were born into this generation by God's appointment. *"From one man he made all the nations, that they should inhabit the whole earth: and he marked out their appointed times in history and the boundaries of their lands"* (Acts 17:26). Recognizing and embracing this truth opens up new frontiers and opportunities not yet imagined. The same Holy Spirit that hovered over the earth on creation's morning desires to ignite our creativity and imagination to things not yet seen or accomplished. What could that mean for you?

On July 13, 2018, I was on the phone with my father who is now eighty-nine years old. He has served God all of his life. We were praying for a harvest of souls when my spirit was caught up into the Lord's presence. In a vision, He took me and suspended me over a wheat field that extended further than my eyes could see. I was about ten feet over this ripened field when suddenly the Lord called for an end-time harvest. As soon as He spoke it, I witnessed an instant response. Immediately, from my peripheral vision, I saw stalks of wheat that were red, yellow, black, and white flying together into huge bundles. These bundles were then bound together by unseen angels. While this happened, the sky over my head opened up like the sky inside the eye of a hurricane. The sheaves that had been gathered were caught up in the force of the whirlwind and spun upward into heaven.

The same Holy Spirit that hovered over the earth on creation's morning desires to ignite our creativity and imagination to things not yet seen or accomplished.

"Lord, this is so easy!" I exclaimed, giddy with excitement over the speed and ease of the great harvest.

"That's because it is time," He replied. "It is time for the end-time harvest."

Just twenty months after showing me this harvest, our church of just over 2,000 people has already seen nearly 800,000 souls come to Christ! God is doing exactly what He said He would do.

Jesus declared, *"This gospel of the kingdom will be preached in the whole world as a testimony to all nations, and then the end will come"* (Matt. 24:14). I believe technology will be the means by which we complete the task. The devil has certainly used it for his kingdom; it's high time we used it for our Lord's.

What is God calling you to do? What opportunity is lurking just around the next corner?

For our ministry, God has called us to pioneer a superhighway for one hundred million souls to travel upon. We are operating under a *100 million souls mandate* that God has given us. Our goal can be reached if one thousand churches win one hundred thousand souls each.

When we consider the enormity of the task left undone, one hundred million souls are only a fraction of what is needed. There are 865 million unreached Muslim or Islamic followers, 550 million unreached Hindus, and 275 million unreached Buddhists. "Two-thirds of the world's population (more than 4.4 billion people) live in what Christian Missions Strategist Luis Bush named, "the 10/40 Window."[3]

This includes the area of North Africa, the Middle East, and Asia approximately between 10 degrees north and 40 degrees north latitude. The 10/40 Window is often called "The Resistant Belt" and includes the majority of the world's Muslims, Hindus, and Buddhists. "Of the fifty-five least evangelized countries, 97% of their population lives there."[4] With our present-day technology, the ability to win 100 million souls out of this window is so doable!

LOW HANGING FRUIT

This goal is also within our reach because we are gathering low hanging fruit. "It is estimated that ninety percent of these unreached people have not been evangelized, with only ten percent of the missionary force working there."[5] But they are ripe and ready to hear the Gospel. Now, through video technology, the global church can partner with Christians located within that window and bring the Gospel to those who have never heard it! We can finally shatter the 10/40 Window!

We went outside of the box to see these results. The same will be true for all who reach the heights of their purpose. Do what others have done if you want similar results; but if you dream of higher achievement, it will require more. Allow our story to ignite new frontiers and ideas for you to explore. Dare to push the limits in your thinking.

Greatness by its very nature is not found in the middle of the curve or graph. Greatness is an extreme, located far from the safe and the mediocre. It requires an abandonment of the predictable and the easy. The crowd of naysayers must be left behind for the lonely path that only a few will follow, and that makes all the difference.

Greatness is an extreme, located far from the safe and the mediocre.

When I traveled to Pakistan to preach to 200,000 people in a Muslim city, I didn't go there because video crusades aren't effective. I traveled there because the Church in the West is full of skepticism. As the Church in America declines, it becomes easy to doubt the reports of the enormous numbers of people coming to Christ overseas. In our part of the world we have seen so little of His miraculous power that it is difficult to believe the testimonies of the notable healing miracles happening in other places. So I traveled there, putting my life at risk, to see it with my own eyes. I wanted to verify the numbers of people coming to Christ and to witness the healing miracles for myself. I needed to be able to say, "I have been there and I am an eyewitness." I had to strike out on a different path.

I was surely not disappointed! While there, I preached a one-night crusade, and over 153,000 Pakistanis received Christ and astonishing miracles happened! It is truly an amazing sight to witness when an enormous crowd of that size stands on their feet to accept Christ! I am an eyewitness that this harvest is real. (You can watch a short video of the crusade at www.wifijesus.org.)

I went there to repeat Peter's words on the Day of Pentecost, *"People of Israel, listen! God publicly endorsed Jesus the Nazarene by doing powerful miracles, wonders, and signs through him"* (Acts 2:22 NLT). This is still true in our day. God is still publicly endorsing His Son through powerful miracles, wonders, and signs.

The healing miracles we have witnessed in our video crusades are astounding. Even the paralyzed and the blind have been healed. Asiimwe Faith, an elderly woman, was paralyzed for three years. Neither the medical doctors nor the witch doctors she visited could help her. In search of a miracle, she attended a video crusade we were conducting in Uganda, and the living Jesus healed her. We witnessed the effects of her miracle on screen as we watched the livestream feed. Asiimwe and many others were ecstatic to share what God had done for them. This once paralyzed woman was able to walk, jump, and praise the Lord! She is just one of the hundreds whom God healed. After each message, we pray for the sick, and people line up to share the miracles they have received.

Little Ruth was a young lady suffering from epilepsy. Each day she suffered multiple intense seizures. She had given up on school or any hope of a normal life, but in one of our internet meetings, God healed her completely! Since then, many more with epilepsy have been healed by the power of God.

We have seen legs, knees, and backs work again. Those who were previously lame jump up and down, eager to show us their miracle. Many with back problems have bent all the way over to touch the ground to demonstrate how God touched them.

During one crusade in Uganda, a middle-aged blind lady was standing in the crowd on the front row. As people came forward to testify how the living Jesus had performed miracles in their bodies, she suddenly began to jump up and down shouting, "I can see! I can see!" Her eyesight was restored in front of the entire crowd of people.

God is still publicly endorsing His Son Jesus with the same kind of miracles we read about in the Gospels, and He is doing them in our video crusades. Parents brought their children forward to show us where tumors and growths have suddenly vanished. These public miracles are bringing hundreds of thousands of people to Christ.

Busigye Judith is a middle-aged lady in East Africa whose friends had to carry her to a recent video crusade. Her knee was swollen for four years, and she was unable to bend it even slightly during all of that time. At the crusade, I shared a previous healing miracle that I witnessed with my own eyes decades earlier. I explained of the time when my wife and I lived in Czechoslovakia after communism fell in Eastern Europe. We traveled there to preach the Gospel and had the opportunity to speak at a crusade in the city of Prague. One night during the crusade, a lady came forward on crutches for prayer. Her knee was swollen to twice its normal size. When she came forward, I told her, "I can't heal you, but tonight I am representing a living Jesus. Because He is alive, He will heal your body and save your soul."

As soon as I spoke those words to the crippled lady, she quit looking at me and started staring at her knee. She completely and utterly believed my words, and because she believed Jesus was going to do what she had requested, she wanted to watch it happen! Seeing her faith ignited my own! I too stopped looking at her face and I started staring at her swollen knee along with her. I wanted to watch it happen too!

As we prayed, her knee was immediately healed. It was like someone stuck a pin in a balloon. Her knee shrunk to its normal size right before our eyes! The next thing that happened was marvelous to behold. She threw down her crutches and started running back and forth in the tent, weeping, shouting, and praising God!

As I shared this testimony decades later in a video crusade in Africa, Busigye Judith placed her hands on her knee and was healed instantly in exactly the same manner! Her knee went to its normal size right in front of her eyes. She too jumped up and down, praising God as she told us her story!

This demonstration of God's miraculous power has been repeated again and again over the last fifteen months. The lame walk, the blind see, and the mute can speak again. While I was in Pakistan, a lady who was unable to speak for seven months came on the stage to tell me that God had healed her. She then left the stage and came back with her adult daughter. She wanted her daughter to confirm that her mother was telling the truth! How wonderful to see both mother and daughter able to speak with one another again!

Most of the miracles I just described happened while I was in my home city here in America. It was all done outside of the lines that had previously been drawn. What creative ideas has God given you?

What creative ideas has God given you?

When we conduct a video crusade, I normally preach the message live through the internet from our campus in Pensacola, Florida. While I preach, our intercessors (who are the real reason for our success) pray. Some are in the same room as me. Others, who are a part of our online campus, pray from their location in various places all around the world. It is a full-on spiritual battle that ensues. Often, we have had the internet connection go down at the most crucial time. That is when our prayer warriors step up their game, and we have seen our connection suddenly reestablished. It may sound like science fiction to you, but they will gladly tell you of the miraculous battles they have won through prayer.

As I preach in Pensacola, a local pastor stands on the stage in his country and translates the message into the people's language. Let me tell you, those translators can preach with fire and anointing! This is all usually done live on both ends with, hopefully, only a small satellite delay.

REMOTE, NO-INTERNET-ACCESS AREAS

In our efforts to go to places where the Gospel has not been preached, we realized that we would be traveling into areas where there was no internet connection or where it was poor at best. It became apparent that we needed a Plan B to reach these remote areas, so we decided to record a "backup message." This was another instance where we had to try something that had never been done before and test something new.

Having a backup message prepared also became necessary because our crusades quickly grew from five to eight thousand people to ten to twelve thousand people, and then to well over 100,000 people. With that many people in attendance, we had to deliver— with or without the internet. We were also spending over $100,000 dollars to fund each large crusade. I felt personally responsible for all the money and energy that was being spent. Local pastors and their church members spent weeks with "boots on the ground," knocking on doors and canvassing villages. They spent weeks away from home with a commitment to souls that I have not seen paralleled anywhere. We couldn't let them down, nor the people who were coming and had never before heard the Gospel.

The message had to be delivered no matter what challenges we encountered, so we brought some of the local pastors we were working with to America and recorded backup video crusade messages. We started that process with the lead pastor and his wife from Pakistan. At our Pensacola campus, with no more than sixty adults in the room, I preached and the pastor's wife translated. We preached as though we were in Pakistan standing before tens of thousands of people. Our media team (some of the other heroes in this story) put video images of the crowds from previous crusades on the back and side screens. Those in the room with us were asked to pray as if they were in Pakistan, in a sea of lost humanity who had never heard the Gospel before. We asked them to earnestly pray because heaven and hell hung in the balance for thousands of souls.

The night we recorded the video, I was on the twenty-third day of a forty-day fast. As I stood up to preach that night the Lord spoke to me, "This is not just a backup message; this will be used to reach hundreds of thousands of people for Christ. This is the real deal, so preach like it!"

What happened next was glorious. The translator and I both felt the power of God touch our words. We moved in perfect tandem as His Spirit flooded the room. We prayed for salvations and miracles and then asked the people to come forward to share what God had done in their lives. It was as if we were there. Those in the room testified of how the anointing that fell that night burned deeply in their hearts.

Would you believe that the next two crusades we conducted in Pakistan had no internet signal! That had never happened before, but God went ahead of us to make a way where there was none.

I believe the creativity of the Holy Spirit allowed us to think outside of the box and it worked! That recorded message, preached with just sixty people in the room, has already reached 174,175 new converts for Christ.

I remember how anxious I was when we used that backup message for the first time. It wasn't what we had planned. We spent $121,000 to rent hundreds of buses, lights, sound equipment, the crusade grounds, and LED screens for that crusade. One hundred thousand people were expected. And then we lost all internet and cellular connection with our team in Pakistan when the scheduled time of the crusade drew near due to the remoteness of the area. Thank God the backup message was available.

Our intercessors prayed and we waited expectantly even though we had no communication and no idea what was happening on their side. It took hours before a cell signal was reestablished and we could again communicate. I felt like the flight controllers in NASA must have felt when the lunar module went to the backside of the moon! Had we spent all this money in vain? Did everything go as planned? Did the miracles still happen and souls get saved? Then, after what seemed like forever, my phone rang. The team had finally been able to receive a cellular signal, but the crusade was over. As I remained on the phone with the Pakistani pastor, his words poured out as he described what had transpired. He was so excited that he was out of breath. "Pastor," he said, "it was unbelievable! The miracles were amazing, and the altar call was mind-blowing!"

I then asked him the question I was so anxious to have answered: "From the response you saw, did the recorded video message work as well as a live crusade?"

"It totally surprised me," he responded. "I had my doubts about this working, but during the recorded message, when you called for the people to stand to their feet to accept Christ, the whole crowd stood with hands raised. And when you prayed for the sick, miracle after miracle began to happen. There were so many healed that we ran out of time before we could get to everyone who came forward to testify."

Our final tally, from this one-night video crusade with a recorded message, was 81,554 decisions for Christ! I believe that God can do even greater things through those who will discover His will, embrace the hour in which they live, and attempt new things. Right now, Holy Spirit-inspired pioneers are in great demand. The volatile time in which we live will be seen by most as just more chaos, but for the savvy it will be viewed as a time of tremendous opportunity. It has created a vacuum that only new creativity can fill. Those who fill the void will understand that change is not an enemy, but rather an ally.

Change is not an enemy, but rather an ally.

I recently shared with an American friend what God was accomplishing through video technology. She was ecstatic at first, but then responded sadly, "Every time we bring up technology in our church, they fight it." Her response should unfortunately not surprise anyone. The church has historically been the very last entity to adapt to a changing world. As a Body, we have fought change. We yield only when the train has already left the station and we must concede. What a pity. The Gospel *message* never changes, but our *methods* of delivering it should always be in step with the generation we are trying to reach. While churches have resisted technology, people are dying without Christ. It is estimated that approximately 66,000 people are dying without any knowledge of Christ every day.[6] They don't have another day to wait! They need the Gospel delivered to them now, through whatever means we have available to us.

New solutions come to those brave, tenacious souls who will not settle for the status quo. One fresh idea from heaven can exponentially expand our horizons. Perhaps you will pioneer the next major breakthrough with the creativity power of the Holy Spirit inside of you!

Our greatest limitation is often found residing between our two ears. An old mind-set must be broken and replaced by the truth that, *"I can do all things through Christ who strengthens me"* (Phil. 4:13 NKJV). Extraordinary results will require something more than ordinary approaches. Often we allow our present environment to blind us to new possibilities.

Extraordinary results will require something more than ordinary approaches.

Earlier, I shared how God caught me up in the Spirit and took me to a vast wheat field to witness an end-time harvest. I want to share with you now the conclusion of what I saw in that vision. While watching the wheat come together from the four corners of the earth, I noticed that none of the wheat from the field I was suspended over was being gathered. That field stretched further than I could see. I was puzzled by this, so I asked the Lord, "What about this wheat, why is none of it being harvested?" He responded, "It's not wheat. It looks like wheat and talks like wheat, but it is not wheat." I was absolutely dumbfounded and shocked! From its outward appearance, it all looked the same.

From the proximity of the wheat field I knew that God was speaking about the American church, and my heart was broken. I echo the words of the prophet Jeremiah:

Oh, that my head were a spring of water and my eyes a fountain of tears! I would weep day and night for the slain of my people (Jeremiah 9:1).

I love my country, and I want her to be saved. I am trusting for a turnaround. But we cannot allow the backsliding of our own nation to blind us to the vast opportunity further from us. We must take Jesus to the other nations now! There are billions in the valley of decision, low-hanging fruit begging to be harvested, with not another day to wait. We have the technology to complete the task, and the time is now!

We cannot afford to fall into the common trap of being blinded by what's right in front of us, missing the potential of what is just out of our reach. Let's look beyond the present and see what can be. God is looking for pioneers to blaze new trails. Those trails will not only pave the way for many to follow but will also take the pioneers who forge them to the desired destination of finding purpose, meaning, and significance in their own personal lives.

NOTES

1. The Billy Graham Library, "When and Where was Billy Graham's Largest Crusade?" accessed April 16, 2020, https:// billygrahamlibrary.org/when-and-where-was-billy-grahams -largest-crusade/.

2. Steve Warren, "'Light the Fire Again' Revival Meetings Aim to Reignite Brownsville, Pensacola Awakenings," CBN News, June 6, 2019. https://www1.cbn.com/cbnnews/cwn/2019/june/ light-the-fire-again-revival-meetings-hope-to-reignite -brownsville-and-pensacola-awakenings.

3. Howard Culbertson, "10/40 Window: Do You Need to be Stirred to Action?" Southern Nazarene University, accessed April 16, 2020, http://home.snu.edu/~hculbert/1040.htm.

4. Ibid.

5. Ibid.

6. Ibid.

CHAPTER NINE

On Mission

W E have already decrypted several clues that will lead you to God's specific will for your life. First, we learned that our destiny is tied to the generation in which we live. We were placed in this generation by God's design. This being the case, we do well to pay special attention to the uniqueness of our era.

Our second discovery is that God's general will for our lives is to serve the purposes of God in our generation and then to fall asleep. God has hardwired us with this desire. Self-doubt will try to extinguish it, but we need to trust God for great things. We were created for greatness.

The next clue is the reality that the greatest opportunities for this generation are intertwined with technology. The most notable difference in this generation from all previous ones is our technology. Today's pioneers don't travel in sailing ships, covered wagons, or rail, but they move with the speed of the internet. The whole world is within our reach.

The fourth breadcrumb we discussed is that greatness requires you to think outside of the box. Pause and reflect on the amazing creativity of our Creator! One trip to the zoo reminds us! Today's technology gifts us with profound opportunities to be creative with never before possibilities. Ask the Holy Spirit to give you creative ideas and to help you think of a new way of doing things.

> *Today's pioneers don't travel in sailing ships, covered wagons, or rail, but they move with the speed of the internet.*

In this chapter, we will reveal perhaps the most missed clue for living a life of purpose, meaning, and joy. Even many Christians have failed to see how critical this piece is to their well-being. They often miss it because they only see the enormous benefit it brings to others, while failing to see the abundant joy it can bring to their own lives.

The reason why many Christians don't experience purpose, meaning, and joy in their lives is because they are not actively engaged in the mission of winning people to Christ. A recent survey revealed the top five things people think of when they hear the word *Christian*. Purpose, meaning, and joy were nowhere on the list. Yet Jesus clearly told us this is why He came. In John 15:11, Jesus said, *"I have told you this so that my joy may be in you and that your joy may be complete."* His aim was for us to live a life of abundant joy, and yet this attribute was not even on the radar when people were asked to describe what it meant to be a Christian.

In the early church there was great joy. A quick glance reveals that those in the early church constantly shared their faith, even in the midst of great persecution. The Bible says, *"Those who had been scattered preached the word **wherever they went**"* (Acts 8:4, emphasis added). They lived their lives and preached Jesus. In other words, they were walking in the initial call of what it means to follow Jesus, as "fishers of men." They lived on mission. The book recording their story is accurately named, "The Acts of the Apostles." They were fishers of men, and that reality resulted in their abundant joy.

When people exchange hell for heaven it is easy to see the benefit they receive by coming to Christ, but there is another tremendous benefit for those who are bringing Christ to them. It is this dynamic that is often missed. Without it, purpose, meaning, and joy become elusive.

Imagine how boring it would be to go to fishing classes every Sunday, week after week, year after year, decade after decade, but never experience the thrill of landing a fish. In the same way, much of the Church has lost its joy because we aren't catching fish. Joy has been replaced with ritual and routine. Let me ask you a question—would you rather go to a fishing class or actually catch some fish?

Our churches are supposed to be vibrant places of community and yet many people attend them without ever experiencing a warm embrace from others or from God. We have become absorbed with our own selves and no longer see the needs of those around us. The passion for souls has all but gone out. This leads to a joyless life.

I believe much of the boredom and lethargy felt by Christians would disappear if we returned to the business of actually winning people to Christ. As Christ-followers, we must get back to Jesus' original invitation to become fishers of men.

As Christ-followers, we must get back to Jesus' original invitation to become fishers of men.

When my son, Christian, was young, I made a plan to take him fishing; I wanted to see his excitement when he actually caught a fish. At that time, I traveled across a long bridge every day to get to work. The bridge was high, and it overlooked a lower causeway. It was very common to see people fishing there, and I began to see a pattern. There was one old beat-up station wagon that was parked in the same spot every day. I concluded that this fisherman must have found the very best fishing hole on the entire causeway!

I told Christian that I had discovered a wonderful fishing spot, but we would need to get up really early to fish there. The night before our trip, we had everything ready. The next morning, we rolled out of bed at some ridiculously early hour, and off we went to haul in the catch!

I was so excited when we arrived because "the spot" was vacant. We set up and cast our lines into the water. I was sure that we would catch fish at any moment, but thirty minutes later, we didn't have even a nibble. I silenced my concerns by reasoning that it was still early, and we just needed to give it a little more time. I absolutely knew we were in the right spot!

That is when I saw that familiar old station wagon approaching. The elderly driver crept by us looking to see who was in his favorite fishing hole. After he passed, I whispered to Christian, "Did you see him looking at us? We are going to catch some fish today!"

Well, the other fisherman parked about fifty yards past us. He baited several fishing poles and threw his lines out into the water. Then, to my surprise, he started walking slowly in our direction. He never once looked back over his shoulder to see if he might be getting a bite. At first, I thought this strange, but then I reasoned that he wasn't expecting to catch any fish, because he was not in the right spot—we were!

The elderly gentleman came down to us and struck up a conversation. He was wearing old coveralls and totally looked the part of a seasoned fisherman, but he never once glanced back to check on his own fishing poles. What was even more surprising was that he didn't seem to have any interest in ours either!

That is when a terrible realization hit me. We gave up sleep that Saturday morning for nothing! It was a big fat bummer! The old fisherman's main goal was not to catch anything; he just loved the experience of fishing. He simply enjoyed hanging out and conversing with other "fishermen." As I looked around at the others dotting the shoreline, I realized they all looked the part, they had their fishing lines baited and in the water, but none of them expected to catch fish! It was just their routine. They had forgotten the joy of the catch. The old fisherman dressed like a fisherman, even talked like a fisherman, but he really wasn't one.

As we pursue happiness, we must be careful not to believe the lie that joy comes from living for our own selfish desires. Every day we receive cultural messages that reinforce a self-serving attitude. Advertisers say, "Life is all about you!" But let's stop and think about the folks we know who are totally self-focused. Can we describe them with words like *joy* or *authentic happiness*? Now let's examine ourselves. In what areas of your life are you most prone to adopt a self-serving attitude? Are you generally the happiest in those areas of your life?

Jesus taught and lived a different way. By His example we are taught to abandon a life of self-gratification for a life of serving others. We are instructed to leave the ninety-nine for the one. We are instructed to:

> *Let nothing be done through selfish ambition or conceit, but in lowliness of mind let each esteem others better than himself. Let each of you look out not only for his own interests, but also for the interests of others. Let this mind be in you which was also in Christ Jesus, who, being in the form of God, did not consider it robbery to be equal with God, but made Himself of no reputation, taking the form of a bondservant, and coming in the likeness of men. And being found in appearance as a man, He humbled Himself and became obedient to the point of death, even the death of the cross* (Philippians 2:3-8 NKJV).

Jesus knew that when we lose our life, we truly find it. When we let go of our own self-interest with our hands wide open, He will fill them anew with much greater blessings. We discover lasting joy by living a radically generous life.

Even the simplest act of generosity can cause great joy. I experienced this in a most unlikely way several years ago when I stopped at a Burger King drive-through for lunch. I had a coupon for a free burger when I purchased another one. I didn't really need two burgers, but because it was free, I accepted it. (Don't judge me, I know I am not the only one!) As I pulled out of the drive-through, I noticed a homeless man standing by the side of the road. I lowered my window and called him over. As he shuffled to the car, I said to him, "Hey man, I have these two burgers that I just got from the drive-through. I can't eat both of them, are you hungry?"

We discover lasting joy by living a radically generous life.

A toothless smile broke out on his face as his eyes lit up as he responded, "Sure! Thanks a lot man." That's when the most amazing and unexpected thing occurred. As I drove off, an overwhelming sense of joy filled my heart as tears rolled down my cheeks. I felt so full of life, such a sense of wholeness and, you guessed it, unspeakable joy! I experienced all of this from giving a burger that had cost me nothing. I honestly can tell you that I cannot remember ever experiencing that same level of joy from anything I have purchased for myself in over fifty years of my existence. It cost me nothing but became priceless. With one simple act of generosity, unbridled joy invaded my heart.

True joy is found in serving. Jesus demonstrated how to live a life of abundant joy. If we could choose only one word to describe the life of Jesus, I think we would have to choose the word *generous*. He gave everything He had for us. *"For you know the grace of our Lord Jesus Christ, that though he was rich, yet for your sake he became poor, so that you by his poverty might become rich"* (2 Cor. 8:9 ESV). Jesus left His home in Heaven, He lived a sinless life, and He died a brutal death—all for you and me. He held nothing back. Generosity was certainly the hallmark of His life, and it is our very best example of how we can discover a life of lasting joy, even in our digital world.

We now live in a technology-driven world vying for our time and attention. The screen holds many in a prison of loneliness as they seek "authentic" relationships amidst inauthentic community. And as we travel this new digital landscape, even modern science is learning that being connected to other people is vital to our overall happiness.

> *The screen holds many in a prison of loneliness as they seek "authentic" relationships amidst inauthentic community.*

When Christopher Peterson, one the founders of positive psychology, was asked to describe in two words or fewer what positive psychology was all about, he replied, "Other people."[1]

Dr. Martin E.P. Seligman, the former president of the American Psychological Association (APA), asserts that, "Today it is accepted without dissent that connections to other people and relationships are what give meaning and purpose to life."[2] He emphatically believes that "there is no denying the profound influences that positive relationships or their absence have on well-being."[3] Dr. Seligman also wrote, "Very little that is positive is solitary. When was the last time you laughed uproariously? The last time you felt indescribable joy? The last time you sensed profound meaning and purpose? The last time you felt enormously proud of an accomplishment? Even without knowing the particulars of these high points of your life, I know their form: all of them took place around other people."[4]

With the advent of the internet and social media, our entire world is connected and operates as a global community, so why are antidepressant drugs a multibillion-dollar industry? The technology that promised us greater access to one another has become for many a disappointing substitute for meaningful relationships. But it doesn't have to be so.

What if I told you that new live video conferencing technology has now opened a door for the most authentic encounters and miracles we could ever experience? Joel Comm, author of the book *Twitter Power 2.0,* gave the most accurate definition of social media that I have read. He defines social media as "content that has been created by its audience."[5] That content contains the dreams, aspirations, and hopes of an entire world. Amazingly, you and I have access to them. Doesn't that sound like an enormous opportunity for the church? We can inject hope into the global conversation that is already taking place. We can lift up Jesus so that He can *"draw all men to Myself"* (John 12:32 NASB).

We have entered into a new era that's been dubbed the Conversational Era. It's time that we recognize that the internet is the greatest opportunity for evangelism today. "Through social media, society is being rearranged fundamentally and at a faster rate than many people realize. Until the Conversational Era came along, people were constrained by geography."[6]

Think of the power of those words. We are no longer "constrained by geography." Think of the amazing potential this truth presents to the Church to fulfill her great commission. The possibilities of a "flat world" are hard to grasp because the implications are enormous. However, through advanced technology all of us can be involved in taking the Gospel to the nations. We can all fulfill our God-given destiny. All of us have the world within our reach. That means we can all live on mission and enjoy the life we always wanted to live—the life of abundant joy!

We cheat ourselves when we believe that God has never given us any shot at doing something great for Him. We have opportunities all around us to share our faith. You see, God uses ordinary people to do extraordinary things in ordinary situations. Many waste time waiting for some big ministry platform, not realizing that there are opportunities to do great things for God all around them. If we are faithful with little, God will give us more. Oh, dear reader, don't wish away your life, don't wait to start living your destiny tomorrow. Become a fisher of men now and discover the purpose, meaning, and joy that accompany being on mission.

The events and stories found within the pages of this book are all true. They are happening in other countries around the world, but they are also happening right here in America to those who are living on mission. All of us can be living our destiny now, right where we are, right where God has planted us.

You were placed in this generation by God's design for greatness. Your destiny is tied to the technological context in which we all live. The measure and the way you engage our new world will ultimately determine the level of joy you experience. Let me show you a way to unlock your potential as never before.

NOTES

1. Martin Seligman, *Flourish* (New York: Free Press, 2011), 20.

2. Ibid, 17.

3. Ibid, 21.

4. Ibid, 20.

5. Joel Comm, *Twitter Power 2.0* (Wiley Publishers, 2010).

6. Shel Israel, *Twitterville: How Businesses can Thrive in New Global Neighborhoods* (Portfolio Publishers, 2009).

CHAPTER TEN

The Joy Secret

THOSE who live in the West live with so much plenty, and yet joy is so scarce. I rarely see it in the airports I travel or on the roads I drive. The frantic pursuit of it is everywhere, and yet is seems almost impossible to find. Yet in other parts of the world, I witness an abundance of joy among those who have very little in material goods.

I saw this joy in a pastor and his wife in Uganda who took a radical step in order to reach their community. They sold their business in order to have money to win the lost. Would you sell your business or your home to fund a crusade to reach the lost? That's pretty out-of-the-box right? That is what this couple did after they attended one of our video crusades. He and his wife immediately decided to sell their cows—their livelihood—to fund an outreach in their hometown, and this radical act of generosity resulted in their overflowing joy. We met them after they attended one of our crusades and pastors' conference in Central Africa. In those meetings we expected hundreds of people to attend, but that number quickly turned into thousands. Soon there were so many coming that we couldn't accommodate all of them. Pastors and leaders joined us from the countries of Sudan,

Tanzania, Uganda, Democratic Republic of Congo, Burundi, and Rwanda. The thirst for God these men and women demonstrated was amazing, and so was their raw joy.

Here is a message I received from our time together with them:

> To the Upward Church family,
>
> Greetings in the mighty name of the Lord!
>
> On behalf of the outreach to East and Central Africa, we want to thank you so much and give you a report upon the recently concluded crusade and conference in Sanga town.
>
> What a power packed three days!
>
> We're so thankful to God for the great work he did in this town and the surrounding villages. It was one of our biggest crusades. We had a turnout of 4,500 people, with 1,568 of these giving their lives to Jesus!
>
> God in a mighty way visited this village. He saved them, healed them, and nightly demonstrated Jesus to be His Son to a village that was full of demon worship. It was shocking when the host pastor, Pastor Noah, called people forward to repent and many in the church were still going to worship Satan or the bachwezi spirits. Over 500 people came forward to confess that they were worshiping both Jesus and satanic spirits!
>
> This village was characterized by witchcraft, but the presence of the Lord touched the hearts of many who were witchcraft followers. They denounced worshiping the devil and gave their lives to Christ. Even some of the

witch doctors who manipulated the people with lies for many years surrendered their witchcrafts and gave their lives to Christ. People brought their idols and charms and we burnt them all in a huge bonfire.

We came back with our hearts singing melodies to the Lord and appreciating His faithfulness! The number of miracles that happened was uncountable. One named Rwakabutemba from Kiruhura was a 75-year-old man who had suffered diabetes for close to 15 years. He was healed instantly when Pastor Craig preached in the crusade in Sanga.

At the same time, two ladies in the gathering who had suffered severe back pain and could not bend over were completely healed. They could not feel any pain anymore and, as a result, gave their lives to Christ.

Among those healed were a paralyzed woman, some other women, and a man who can now move with ease! Praise the Lord! There are so many testimonies still coming in!

God richly bless you, Upward family, for doing life with us! Continue praying for these people and the pastors who are doing follow-ups! It's our heart's desire that we would equip them with a copy of the Bible and a copy of *Last Minute God* to help them walk in their journey.

We are so thankful that God endorsed His Son through signs and wonders. May God richly bless you! Looking forward to doing life together in the next village of Biguri.

God bless you,

Muhanguzi Gideon

May I repeat one of the phrases from this letter? "We came back with our hearts singing melodies to the Lord." This is the joy of which I speak.

It was during this crusade that God did a deep work within the pastor and his wife mentioned at the beginning of the chapter. They live in a remote part of Uganda. As they watched 1,568 people come to Christ in those meetings, it ignited a fresh fire within them. They immediately wanted to share in the vision to reach 100 million souls for Christ, so they went home and sold their cattle (their livelihood) to help fund a video crusade in their area. They wanted God to move in their villages in the same way that they had just witnessed in Sanga town. They didn't wait for others to join them to get it started; they just went home and sold their cattle!

The response we received to the outreach that they helped fund was so incredible that once again we couldn't accommodate all of the people. They slept in schools, tents, and on the ground. Some walked for days to attend the meetings. They just kept coming!

Their hunger for God drove them past their natural hunger. We planned on feeding those who attended the four days of the outreach, but the crowd grew so rapidly that we could only promise one meal a day. Even this did not deter them. The crowd kept growing.

Their hunger for God drove them past their natural hunger.

I envisioned what their one meal a day would look like from my American mind-set. I guess I imagined something like a potluck meal at a church function. My sumptuous American image of their one meal a day quickly vanished when I was sent a video of the meal actually prepared for them. It consisted of a giant mound of green bananas and a big pile of large sweet potatoes. For four days, thousands came so hungry for Jesus that they were content to live on one bowl of porridge consisting of green bananas and sweet potatoes. This was their one meal for the day, and yet in the midst of their great lack, there was so much joy!

The believers who prepared the meals smiled, laughed, and talked as they washed plastic dishes in water they had carried to their open-air makeshift kitchen. They cooked the porridge in large pots over open fires in a large field. What radiated from them was joy! These were a people on mission, experiencing the abundant joy Jesus came to give.

In our country, if the church coffee bar is not fully stocked, church leadership will probably receive a complaint on a connect card. Often the music is too loud, too soft, too new, too old. If the weather is overcast, it becomes a good reason for many to sleep in and stay home from church. It doesn't even need to be raining anymore to deter us from attending. All of this is what happens when you abandon the mission of winning souls. It then becomes all about us. What's in it for me? And that life deflates the joy out of our lives. This is the spiritual environment that we often experience in America, and it is easy to cast that same shade on other nations. But our spiritual dearth is not theirs.

You can hear the joy of these people from an email I received from one of the pastors helping us.

Dear servants of the most high God!

Shalom to you all, I bring you warm greetings, prayers, and appreciations from the crusade grounds! People who are born again and non-born again have joined us and are working with us for the success of this meeting. I have not seen this kind of expectation and anticipation in the hearts of men like we're experiencing here! They have been so thrilled to see for the very first time pastors of born-again faith coming together to do a Gospel campaign. This has never happened in their area. The Body of Christ is coming together and raising the banner of the Lord! We already have enough space to accommodate 4,000 residents. This area has greatly welcomed Jesus. People are so desperate for Him. They have suffered great loss to the enemy and they are now surrendering to Jesus! The atmosphere is already charged; Christ's visitation is the talk of all the towns near and around!

The intercessors here are doing a great job; from Sunday until the end of the crusade (Saturday night) they will be sleeping in the stadium, praying for the meeting. They are praying for the salvation of many souls and for signs and wonders!

How refreshing! It is no wonder that God is moving there! I am so happy to report that God responded to the hunger of these people. Over 7,500 people showed up in this remote area of Africa and 5,500 people accepted Christ! They gave up food and ate the Bread of Heaven! They gave up shelter and found the Prince of Peace!

The pastor who sold his cows to initiate these meetings wept for the entire four days. He wept so much that the others became concerned. When they checked to make sure he was OK, Pastor Emmanuel responded:

> I was saved at a very young age. As a young man I witnessed powerful healing miracles, and I gave my heart to the Lord. In 1956, God promised me that I would see His power displayed once again, and it would cause a great revival. I can't stop weeping because I have been waiting for this day for such a long time, and now it has come. I never imagined that God would use a white man in America, on a video screen, to bring this revival that He promised to me so long ago. My tears are tears of joy!

The following is the report we received from this district after these meetings concluded:

Gospel Crusade and Conference in Biguri Kamwenge District 22–25th May 2019

To the Upward Church family,

Greetings in the name of our Lord and Savior Jesus Christ, the Lord of the harvest!

With a lot of joy and delight, I bring you brotherly greetings from the saints in Kamwenge, Kyegegwa, Fort Portal, Kyaka, and Kasese districts that gathered in the Biguri-Kamwenge grounds.

We have witnessed four power-packed and life-transforming days and nights in the presence of the Lord! Our hearts are filled with joy for the great work that the Lord did in the lives of the hundreds of pastors and their wives in the conference and the crusade. Kamwenge district is one of the remote areas with biting poverty and very backward practices. It's very deep in the villages with no electricity. The government has just given them running water.

Due to high levels of illiteracy and ignorance in the area, the enemy had made this place a stronghold. Lots of barbaric practices like child sacrifices, idol worship, witchcraft, and other evils of the sort were the order of the day.

According to Bishop Byensi Godwin, they have lacked spiritual support due to the remoteness of the area. None of the pastors from the major cities or evangelists would come to support them with a Gospel meeting and crusade like we just had! This crippled and weakened the church in this area. In so many instances, the church had compromised. It was in a state of slumber, to the extent that some leaders and their flocks were playing double standards, one leg in church and another in the world. They would try the power of God, and if it delays then try witchcraft! We are so thankful to God who made a way where there seemed to be none.

The people were so desperate that many had given up. But now they are rekindled and recommitted to the Lord.

We left the church aligned, back on track, and with their candles burning again!

I, therefore, wish to convey a vote of thanks to Pastor Craig and the entire Upward family for your willingness and obedience to the Lord to reach into the deepest areas of our country where even the local pastors were hesitant to go, thinking that there was nothing good that can come from there! Of all the areas we have been to, this remains the outstanding area that badly and desperately needed the Gospel!

The pastors' conference was historical and marked a turning point in the lives of many pastors. According to the local bishops of the area, "If there are any people who can identify with the message that God chooses those who have failed, those who are not qualified, and those who have given up, it's these people." They were so thankful that God despises no one!

Many people came to witness if indeed God has the power to heal and deliver the demon possessed. One pastor reported, "I am so happy to confidently report that no single person was disappointed!" God healed and delivered so many of them! All of the leaders, both Christians and nonbelievers, were blessed to see the demonstration of God's power in the lives of people! That particular video crusade yielded a total of 5,500 decisions for Christ.

I have received many reports just like this one. They confirm that many nations are filled with people who are desperately hungry for Jesus, and those who are engaged in reaching them are full of joy.

In the same week of this crusade, nearly 100,000 people came to Christ on three different continents through our efforts. This all occurred through the means of today's video technology allowing us to work together with the local believers. If a church our size can win these numbers, imagine what churches that are much larger than ours, with much more resources, can achieve! Imagine what joy it would bring them! I am beyond excited about the staggering results that larger churches will enjoy as they join us in using today's technology with their many resources and contacts.

The American church must get back to the driving passion of actually catching fish. According to Dr. David C. Laubach, the Associate Executive Director of the American Baptist Home Mission Societies, "75% of churches in the United States are plateaued or declining and 24% are growing because they are poaching new members from those declining churches. Only 1% of U.S. churches are growing because they are reaching the unchurched population."[1]

Some might push back and say, "The fish just aren't biting!" My response is, "Go where there are!" That is exactly what serious fishermen do. Have you ever gone fishing with one? If you don't catch something very quickly, they are changing baits and lures. They are trying different techniques, and if the fish don't cooperate quickly, they will tell you to reel in your line because they take off to another spot.

The real problem is we've learned to be content with the experience of fishing while never actually catching any. We enjoy the outing, but actually seeing someone come to Christ is viewed as a bonus, not the objective. We enjoy hearing how to be blessed in our own lives with little care for the souls of others.

I have three older brothers. When we were young, we often went fishing with my cousin, uncle, and dad. If too much time elapsed without anyone catching a fish, we quickly found other ways to occupy ourselves. But as soon as someone caught a fish, everyone perked up. Suddenly our attention was back to catching fish as we cast our lines into the water—usually in the exact spot where the last fish was caught!

The real problem is we've learned to be content with the experience of fishing while never actually catching any.

When we quit actually catching fish, it's easy to forget how much fun it really is. Have you ever seen this happen in a church? Churches are much more exciting when people are consistently coming to the Lord.

We are called to catch fish, but I fear that many just go through the routine. Winning people to Christ is what *all* Christ-followers have been called to do. Every Christian should be engaged in the process, and all of us should be asking, "Have I, or has the church I am a part of, seen anyone come to Christ lately?" Too many churches can go for months, even years, without seeing one person come to Christ in their services with little or no concern.

It is every Christian's responsibility to preach Christ to their world. The apostle Paul wrote, *"Because we understand our fearful responsibility to the Lord, we work hard to persuade others"* (2 Cor.

5:11 NLT). Paul called it a fearful responsibility to persuade others. The prophet Ezekiel wrote:

> *But if the watchman sees the enemy coming and doesn't sound the alarm to warn the people, he is responsible for their captivity. They will die in their sins, but I will hold the watchman responsible for their deaths* (Ezekiel 33:6 NLT).

We have a fearful responsibility because we now know there is a real hell to shun and a real heaven to gain. God says:

> *If I warn the wicked, saying, "You are under the penalty of death," but you fail to deliver the warning, they will die in their sins. And I will hold you responsible for their deaths* (Ezekiel 3:18 NLT).

This is our great and fearful responsibility to bear. We should be deeply alarmed if we are in a church that never sees anyone come to Christ. If that is the case, I encourage you, go find one that does and serve in it! Whatever we do, we need to fulfill our responsibility.

Earlier, I wrote of how Pastor Emmanuel sold his cows to partially fund one of our crusades. When I learned of their sacrifice, I made a commitment to buy his cattle back for him. I agreed to pay for his cows before I knew how much they cost. I was shocked to learn that they cost $4,166 U.S. dollars! This is a huge amount of money in Uganda. Their willingness to pay such a high cost demonstrates how committed Pastor Emmanuel and his wife were to the harvest. They were committed to winning souls and the joy it brings.

When we informed Pastor Emmanuel that we were ready to send the funds to replace his cattle, he sent the following response back to us through our pastor there. I have included the entire letter so that you could see the commitment of these wonderful people and the joy they are experiencing.

Dear Pastor Noah Kamanzi,

Receive our warm greetings in the name of our Lord Jesus Christ on behalf of all the bishops, pastors, their wives, and the entire Body of Christ from Kamwenge and the neighboring districts of Kyegegwa, Fort Portal, Kasese, and Kyaka districts that attended this historical revival.

We are so much indebted to God and to you. After so many years, God performed a miracle, and our region was able to host an international conference and crusade. Our minds never conceived the joy, fire, and excitement ignited in our hearts. It continues to burn and shine even brighter!

May God richly bless you and increase you for your Christ-like mind and heart that you did not despise us, but honored us and accepted our invitation to come into an area that so many have despised. They could never find a reason to come, but you dearly blessed our hearts and we are so thankful.

Kindly pass our infinite thanks to Pastor Craig for sacrificing all he had to pioneer a revival in an area like ours. We are so very thankful that God used him to restore the church in our region! You guys have pioneered a revolution that will sweep all the surrounding villages and towns! We are so excited that we were able to witness miracles happening with our very eyes, and the heathens who were disrespecting our God saw His power and believed again!

The words pastor shared from America cut us deep into our hearts and our lives; ministries will never be the same again! We are very happy and we thank you!

The people that the Lord saved over the crusade continue to come and fellowship.

We managed to get a place that we hire, and we rent our tents and chairs for our meetings. We bless the name of the Lord for this miracle that drew thousands of people to the Lord and rejoice that they are continuing to come and fellowship!

I'm so thankful for the book that you gave us at the pastors' conference in Mbarara, *Last Minute God*. It has been a great resource.

I want to end by conveying a vote of thanks to Pastor Craig for such a generous heart of thinking and promising to refund the money that I spent when I sold my cows to support the crusade. May God richly bless him.

However, I will need your advice, Pastor Noah, as I had dedicated these cows to the work of the Lord.

Kindly advise me how to go about this, because after I talked with you, I shared with my wife and we prayed about it. We feel the Lord asking us to give this money for His work. If we are to be refunded this money, we want to use it in purchasing our own chairs and tents. We want to make a temporary shelter on this land that we are renting. We also believe God for the purchase of our church land, so I have agreed with my wife to give this money to the service of the Lord!

I hope you can explain this to Pastor Craig and he allows us to do that and partakes of the blessing of what the Lord is doing in this area!

Allow me to end by sharing the testimony of a miracle that happened to a girl with epilepsy. I got a phone call from the school's headmaster telling me how much he appreciated what we did here. It's now been five days and the young lady has not had a seizure since! She is completely healed and we bless the Lord!

Thank you again, receive all of our love from Kamwenge and all the pastors from this district.

Pastor Emmanuel Rutera

Biguri Full Gospel Church

Those are the words of a man committed to the harvest, of one committed to catching fish. He sold his livelihood to buy bait! He wanted the joy of seeing people come to Christ more than he wanted his cows.

Since that time, Pastor Emmanuel has not only planted one church, but is now planting four more, because in his own words, "We found four good shade trees where we need four more churches." He has found some more fishing holes!

Don't be blinded by the backslidden condition of our own nation and fooled into thinking that the fish aren't biting. The nations are hungry and waiting to hear the Good News. The real question is, who will respond to their call? Will you just *look* like a fisherman, or will you *be* one? Will you experience the joy that accompanies the catch? Will God's watermark be visible in you?

NOTE

1. Craig Walker, *Catch: The Art of Fishing for Souls* (Pensacola: Upward Publishing, 2010), 88.

CHAPTER ELEVEN

The Witch Doctors Came

DO you want your whole life to be characterized by fullness of joy? We learned from a previous chapter that only those who are living on mission experience the abundant joy Jesus came to give. The level of fulfillment and purpose we experience in this life is forever bound to the mission.

Joy comes from winning people to Christ, and the method Jesus used to gather the crowds is still the most effective. Peter stood up on the Day of Pentecost and declared, *"People of Israel, listen! God publicly endorsed Jesus the Nazarene by doing powerful miracles, wonders, and signs through him, as you well know"* (Acts 2:22 NLT). This is still the most effective method to reach the masses.

Let me tell you the story of Sharifa Bibi, a woman who was paralyzed on the left side of her body for eleven months. She was healed instantly on May 11, 2019, at a crusade in Pakistan. She now has full use of her left side, and the miracle God performed in her body convinced many others to receive Jesus Christ as their Lord. God still uses miracles to convince the world that Jesus is His Son, the Savior of the world!

One of the most amazing miracles that I witnessed happened in Tanzania. I still remember how intimidated I felt when I heard the reports of how many people planned to attend my first crusade there. The preparations went better than anyone hoped, and each week I received reports of the enlarged numbers they expected.

Each day, as the trip drew closer, I grew less and less confident that I was the right person for the job. I remember going outside and praying as I looked up at the night stars. "Lord, are You sure You have the right guy? It's just little old me down here."

On that night, the Lord spoke to me right away. He reminded me of what He said in the Gospel of Mark:

> *And these signs shall follow them that believe; In my name shall they cast out devils; they shall speak with new tongues; they shall take up serpents; and if they drink any deadly thing, it shall not hurt them; they shall lay hands on the sick, and they shall recover* (Mark 16:17-18 KJV).

The Lord then said to me, "Craig, can you at least just go over there and lay your hands upon a few sick people? That is all I need you to do. The rest is up to Me." As He spoke those words to me, I envisioned myself doing nothing more than just laying my hands upon the shoulders of the sick in Africa.

"Yes, Lord, I can do that," I answered.

And the Lord replied, "OK, that's the deal. You do your part, and I'll do Mine. You go, and I will take care of the rest."

After that conversation, all the self-imposed pressure came off. I rested in God. That is, until the first night of the crusade!

"You do your part, and I'll do Mine."

When I arrived in Tanzania, I was scheduled to have the first evening to rest from my travels, but it was not to be. Instead, some very excited African pastors and former international students met me at the airport. They told me the crowds had formed for days before the crusade. The night before my arrival one of our students stood up and preached to them, and many gave their lives to Jesus. The people were full of faith, excited, and expecting me to speak to them in just a few short hours! Now at that point I had gone thirty hours without sleep. I didn't sleep on any of my flights, though I tried.

The team took me to my hotel room and said they would be back in an hour to pick me up. I was so exhausted and disoriented that I knew I had to stay awake if I was going to preach that night. I took a cold shower, got dressed, and sat upright on the bed. In a valiant effort to stay awake I sat with both feet on the ground with my back against the wall, but exhaustion took over, and I fell asleep in a sitting position.

The next thing I knew, someone was banging on my door. When I opened the door, the team whisked me down to the lobby. When we left the hotel, I was so dazed that I barely knew my own name. It wasn't much better by the time we pulled into the field packed with people.

When I saw the crowd, I thought, "Great, I finally get the opportunity that any preacher worth his salt would give his right arm for, and I'm so exhausted that I can't think." I comforted myself with the thought that when the worship music started, I would wake up. But it didn't happen. I thought surely I would wake up when I began to preach, but it didn't happen. Honestly, I don't remember what I said in the first part of that message, but I can definitely tell you what I said at the end. The boldness that came over me startled me out of my numbing fatigue as my voice rose to a shout.

"I did not come here preaching a dead Jesus! If He is dead, He cannot heal your body and save your soul. Jesus is alive, and His grave is empty! If you will come to Him tonight, Jesus will heal you and give you eternal life." I looked out over the vast crowd and continued, "I want everyone who is sick and needs a miracle to line up right here." Suddenly, I was wide awake!

The very first person in line for prayer that night was paralyzed. She was in a fetal position. Five ladies actually carried her to the front of the stage, two on each side and one in the back. Her mouth moved up and down continually. It made a clicking sound that reminded me of the sound a skull makes when the upper and lower jaw are repeatedly snapped together. Her eyes were rolled back in her head, and you could only see the whites of her eyes. She didn't know where, or who, she was. All the muscle was gone from her limbs, and when they carried her up to the stage, she was just an emaciated shell of a person.

I remember exactly how long the walk was off of the stage that night to where they held this lady. As I slowly made my way to her, I thought to myself, "How did I get into this?" I was hoping that the first person I prayed for that night would have something minor, perhaps like a headache. But no, I get the hardest case ever!

As I approached this poor lady, I looked up into the sky and silently prayed, "Lord, You remember the deal we made in America.

I told You I didn't feel qualified to come, but You said if I would just come and lay my hands on the sick, You would do the rest. So, Lord, I'm not going to say even a word; I don't want to mess this up. I'm simply going to lay my hand on her shoulder and trust You to do the rest. Please, Lord, show these people that Your Son Jesus is alive."

That was it. That was all the faith I had. That was all I had to give. And when my hand touched her shoulder, she immediately stood straight up. The ladies who carried her to the front gasped in amazement. They fell back as they watched her body straighten right before our eyes. Muscles instantly came on her limbs and she coughed. As she did, a terrible odor came out of her mouth, and a foul green spirit came out with it. Instantly, her jaw quit moving up and down, and her eyes rolled back down in her head.

The crowd was hushed in amazement. She stood their perfectly healed, looked me right in the eyes, totally in her right mind. I fixed my eyes on hers and said to her through the translator, "Would you like to know Jesus who just set you free?"

She nodded and said, "Yes." I then led her in a prayer of repentance and acceptance of what Jesus did for her at the cross.

When we were through praying, she started jumping up and down with her hands in the air. She was shouting something over and over again. "What is she saying? What is she saying?" I asked the interpreter.

"She is shouting, 'I'm free, I'm free! Jesus has set me free!'" he responded. I could never be able to put into words the joy everyone experienced that night! I asked the African pastor to give her a microphone and put her up on the stage. I wanted her to tell the people what Jesus had just done for her.

As she started to walk up onto the stage, I saw another woman burst through the crowd. She literally knocked people out of her way and ran straight for me! I didn't know if I should run or stay. She didn't stop until she was directly in front of me, totally out of breath. Once she caught her breath, she said, "I wasn't even a part of this meeting. I was on my way to the hospital with an abscessed tooth. My jaw was swollen out to here." She then showed us with her hands how far it was swollen. She went on to describe the miserable pain she experienced.

"I normally wouldn't have taken this route to the hospital," she explained. "I don't even know why I chose to come this way, but when I was traveling by this field, I walked by your speakers. When you said the name of Jesus, my jaw returned to normal in size and all the pain left my body. Jesus has healed me! Jesus has healed me!" she shouted.

Those around us who heard her testimony stared at her in amazement. I shouted to the pastors, "Praise God! Give her a microphone and put her up on the stage as well! Let everyone know that Jesus is alive!"

As you can imagine, the crowd went crazy at those two miracles. Everyone in the town knew the lady who had been paralyzed. When they saw her healed, whole, and in her right mind, they saw real proof that Jesus is indeed alive. Then following nights, the crowds grew exponentially and many came to Christ.

On my last day in the city, I preached in a local church. At one point during the message, I looked down and saw that same lady sitting on the front row with eight members of her family. She was smiling from ear to ear. That is the living Jesus whom I preach and the joy that He gives.

Each week we receive new reports of healing miracles taking place. Today, I spoke with a pastor in Pakistan who told me of a lady with throat cancer whom God totally healed in our last meeting. Another report came in this week from Africa, "God healed Mama Lydia who suffered from severe headaches for ten months. The doctors were unable to help her, but Christ has set her free!" And another pastor reported this week that, "Mellon was healed of severe abdominal pains that she has suffered from for the last six months." We have often heard the phrase, "miracles are the dinner bell to salvation." It is true. These healing miracles preceded thousands who are now turning to Christ.

Miracles are the dinner bell to salvation.

Jaja Rose was a witch doctor from the interior of Uganda before she met Jesus. She was engaged in child sacrifices and devil worship. When Jaja witnessed the power of God healing people, she opened her heart to Christ and was gloriously saved. Jaja became a modern-day "woman at the well." When the surrounding villages heard that she had come to Christ, they came to see for themselves what God had done. This is the report we received:

> Today's service at VOL was colorful and interesting. We had close to twenty new people who came to see the leader of witches who gave her life to Jesus. Her testimony

touched everyone. We are glad that today seven people gave their lives to Jesus, praise the Lord.

The team discovered through their follow up with Jaja Rose that the witch doctors in that community had convinced thirty-three families to each offer up one of their children as a human sacrifice so they would receive peace, prosperity, good marriages, protection, good luck, and fertility. She reported there were eight witch doctors still practicing child sacrifices in that community. Through Sister Jaja, we received news that at least thirty children were being held in isolation and would be sacrificed by the witch doctors in ritual worship in an upcoming demonic festival. When we were made aware of this here in America, we asked the pastors there to do everything they could to rescue them. We made a commitment to feed and house those children until they could be placed in homes. The pastors made an appointment with the police, and arrangements were made to rescue the children. We actually prayed with them on a video call the very day they were driving to the location to save the children.

Here is the report we received from that fateful night:

> It was last night that we took a step to save these children's lives by faith. We are glad to let you know that the kids are safe at our rescue home. Friends, we are so grateful for your prayers, for we found other children as well who had been kidnapped from Northern Uganda. They were underway to be sold to Kampala for sacrifice very soon. We expected to find 30 kids according to the information we had, but we found 35 kids and rescued them all!

Jaja took one of the pastors working with us to the bloodied pit where she had taken part in sacrificing children. The pastor sent me photos of the pit and all the strange items used in this demonic worship, such as squirrel heads and human body parts. Jaja confessed that her family members would come late at night, after the parents had left, to take the little bodies and bury them in the bush. The next morning, they would take the parents to the site and tell them, "See, the gods have accepted your sacrifice and taken your children. You have found their favor."

Friend, this is the level of darkness that we are fighting. These people need Jesus, and we now have the technology to come alongside the local church to take Jesus to them. We must answer the call!

Jaja's whole village now knows the great redemption that is found in Christ. Since her conversion, we have conducted a video crusade in that very village, and hundreds more have come to Christ including other witches who have since burned their witchcraft tools, books, and idols.

Jaja traveled and shared her story of what Jesus did for her to seventy-nine families in another village called Rwakobo. Because of her boldness to expose the lies of the witch doctors and the horrors of child sacrifices, her testimony has now resulted in the rescue of an additional forty-two children and the multiple arrests of witch doctors! We have learned that the witch doctors not arrested have fled the area and the child sacrifices have stopped! Jaja was saved to wake up many people who were going to hell. You were saved for the same reason.

God is still using healing miracles for the means of evangelism today. As I share these testimonies of healing miracles with people here in America, I see great relief on the faces of Christ-followers. Their reactions remind me of a drowning man breaking through the surface of the water, gasping for air, and receiving it just in the nick of time. This is the reaction I see over and over again. It is like a breath of hope being inhaled. The church in the West has suffered so many setbacks, seen so little of His power, and witnessed so few of His healing miracles that when they hear these reports and view the crusade videos, you can visibly see hope spring anew in their hearts.

God still endorses His Son Jesus as the true Savior of the world with signs, wonders, and miracles. Hold on to hope, because He is the last-minute God!

I pray the same is happening inside of you as you read these reports. Miracles still happen today! Trust God for your miracle. Allow your hope to be renewed. God still endorses His Son Jesus as the true Savior of the world with signs, wonders, and miracles. Hold on to hope, because He is the last-minute God!

There are many counterfeits in the world today, but only Jesus has all the power, both in heaven and on earth. We can rejoice that through miracles, the Father is showing the nations that Jesus is truly the living Son of God.

CHAPTER TWELVE

Final Word

THERE are two passions that drive my life. The first is that all those who have never heard the Gospel will hear it at least one time in their lifetime. This book was written from a deep, never-sleeping, ever-pressing passion to see more people in heaven. I pray its words stir you so deeply that your life will be exhausted and emptied out for the sake of impacting eternity.

There is such great joy in the journey of following Christ as a fisher of men. There is wonder and awe for all engaged in the mission of winning people to Christ. I pray you will live your life for souls, to plunder hell and populate heaven. I pray that you will press into your God-given destiny.

The second passion is to help everyone I can to live the best life they can possibly live. I hope that I have shown you that both of these passions are inseparable and immutably bound to one another. Our total surrender to God will bring unfathomable results. It requires fasting and prayer, sacrifice and service, giving and faithfulness; but when such conditions are met, God makes this offer, *"Only ask, and I will give you the nations as your inheritance, the whole earth as your possession*" (Ps. 2:8 NLT). All that is left to do is to simply ask and believe.

Surrender to God will bring unfathomable results.

The life we all desire has been laid out in this book. My own pursuit of such a life has brought me abundant joy, significance, and great purpose. I am confident it will do the same for you as you visibly display His watermark.

CHAPTER THIRTEEN

Come on Board

WHEN our church started moving toward reaching 100 million souls through video crusades, it ignited a fire in thousands of pastors, bishops, and church leaders. Many of them committed to join us in our efforts when they saw our forward momentum.

Pastor Noah Kamanzi started with us by being my translator for our video crusades in Uganda. Currently he is conducting crusades in the remotest parts of Africa in partnership with us. Prior to a recent crusade, local witch doctors spent all night sacrificing blood to their gods in hopes that the meetings would fail. Pastor Noah made us aware of this situation, so we immediately enlisted the prayers of our global intercessors. We know the battle is always won in prayer! It is because of our prayer warriors that we have a track record of so many victories. This case with the witch doctors was no exception.

This is the initial report we received back from the crusade Pastor Noah was conducting:

> The enemy lost the first battle when the crusade and con-
> ference happened; this was the first success. Over 400

people have offered their lives to Jesus! Three witch doctors and sorcerers have confessed Christ; one was among the team that was fighting the crusade. The power of the Lord found her in her house and struck her. She was carried to the crusade and confessed Christ! She gave her life to the Lord and surrendered over 25 kids she was keeping in her shrines. She was going to sacrifice them!

The following photos are of some of the children mentioned above with Pastor Noah. These children would no longer be alive today if he had not left what was comfortable to obey God. I pray as you look at the children in this photo that you will come to the conclusion that doing nothing is not an option.

Pastor Noah with the children rescued from occultic sacrifice.

Nineteenth century philosopher John Stuart Mill said, "Bad men need nothing more to compass their ends, than that good men should look on and do nothing."[1]

May that not be said of our lives, or of this generation.

While this video crusade in Uganda was taking place, in real time, a pastor working with Pastor Noah messaged us these words:

> It's one of the most notable and phenomenal miracles that is going to spread all over! We are praying for wisdom in how to protect this former wizard who has come to the Lord and where to take these children, because some of them have been stolen from faraway places. I feel the Lord brought us here for the redemption and the rescue of these precious lives! We need advice! Pray for us

Pastor Noah with the children along with the former witch doctor who gave her heart to Christ.

and for Pastor Noah as he engages with the government officials over the fate of the children and the wizard. We feel she deserves mercy since she has run into the hands of the Father, but the government thinks otherwise! The miracles have pulled in the entire village and the place is packed to capacity right now.

As soon as Pastor Noah was freed from his responsibilities, he sent us this wonderful praise report and an impassioned plea for others to join us in our mission. I wanted you to read this, in his own words, so you can feel the impact of how desperately Jesus is wanted and needed in other countries. Here is his message:

> Every day hundreds of kids are at risk to lose their lives to merciless people who just want their organs and their blood as sacrifices to their gods. It's even hard to believe it with your heart, but such evil things are still practiced here. Africa needs the Savior! Things like this are even not good. We need Jesus. Friends, Satan is continuing to spread his lies and putting people under captivity, but we all know that Christ was revealed to destroy the works of the devil.
>
> We are grateful to the government of Uganda that has recognized the impact that the Gospel is creating. They themselves have begun to arrange conferences and Gospel campaigns to promote the name of Jesus.
>
> Would you also respond to the call of God upon our country as we declare the Kingdom of God to our land?

Friends, we would like to ask you to please stand with us as we lead every tribe, every group, to Jesus. We have answered a call to reach 100 million souls for Jesus! We would like to ask you to be part of this!

Friend, God wants to use *you* to reach people just like this. We are taking the Gospel to where there is grave-worship and child sacrifices to demon spirits. We are taking the Gospel to villages where witch doctors walk the streets and terrorize the people as they display human hands and body parts that they have cut off of their victims. They do this to intimidate others from giving their hearts to Christ.

And yet, the people still come.

A lost world has a deep, heartfelt desire for the Gospel. There are those in our own country with this same desire. Will you find the abundant joy that accompanies the joy of seeing others come to Christ?

Will you come with me on this journey? Let me share with you several immediate opportunities that are available.

1. BIBLES AND OTHER RESOURCES

The following pictures are of the old tattered Bibles that we typically see in Africa. There are so few available that one is shared by many. The people are hungry for God and deeply desire and need a Bible of their own. It costs $8.50 for a new Bible. Will you help us provide the Word of God in their own language? You can give directly at wifijesus.org.

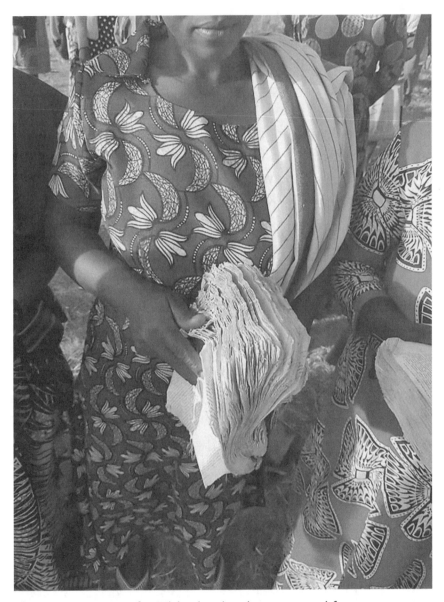

The worn portion of a Bible that has been passed from one believer to another.

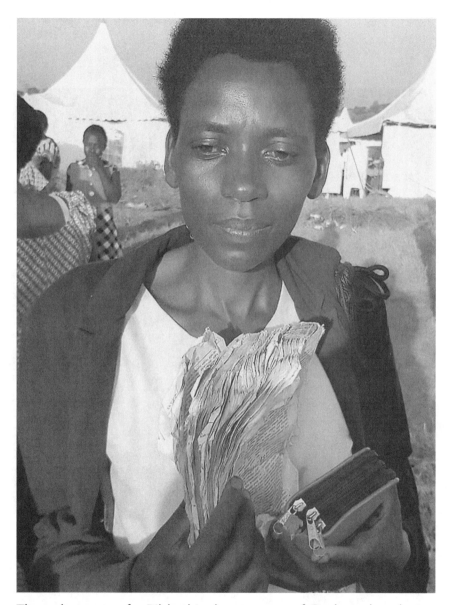

The only pages of a Bible this dear woman of God used to share her faith with her entire village.

179,000 people inside the stadium and over 200,000 both inside and out, hearing the Gospel for the first time in Pakistan during Ramadan.

The number of new converts arising from these video crusades is enormous, and as a result so is the need for books and resources to help these new believers become established. A few years ago, I wrote a book entitled *Last Minute God*. We have had tens of thousands of requests for this book as a Bible study resource. It has been translated into five languages. Will you help us place this book in the hands of thousands of new believers?

The cost of one book in their language is only $2.50. It is an important message that teaches that no matter what type of problem we may face there is hope. It is filled with stories from the Bible to show example after example of how God comes through—often at the very last minute.

Also, if you would like a copy of *Last Minute God* you can receive a copy with a donation of any amount at wifijesus.com.

In Pakistan the need for Bibles is so great that we are working to give one Bible for every ten families! For $6.50 we can place a Bible in Pakistan where it is desperately needed. You can help us to do that by going to wifijesus.org and making a donation. For the price of a designer cup of coffee you can purchase one Bible that will be shared by ten families.

2. SLAVES BOUGHT OUT OF SLAVERY

We are also taking the Gospel to families still held in modern-day slavery. These slaves work in the brick kilns of Pakistan. I visited one of these kilns and witnessed where the slaves are held with their families. Afterward I visited with a former slave family for

Brick kiln family bought out of slavery.

whom we facilitated their freedom by paying off their debt (pictured above). They lived in slavery for eighteen years and their debt was only $2,500. These two boys never went to school. When you are in slavery, everyone in the family, including children and grandparents, must work from sunrise to sunset making bricks in extreme weather. They only make enough for one meal a day and have little hope of ever being free again. Most of these families were put into this situation because they had medical costs that they could not pay. Typically, for $2,500 you can set an entire family free from years of servitude. If you want to release a family from slavery you can do so by giving at wifijesus.org. You can receive more information about these families and actually choose the family that you would like to set free by going to our website.

3. JOIN US

Giving is not the only way you can be involved. We would love first and foremost for your church or ministry to replicate what we are doing, to join us in our march to reach *100 million souls*. We would love to assist them in any way we can. If they have questions or need more information, please contact us at wifijesus.org. Please pass this book on to your leader and tell them what it has meant to you. *We are trusting God for 10,000 churches to join us.*

If the church you are part of chooses not to join this effort, but you still want to be a part, check out our online experience. You can be a part of the prayer team. There are opportunities to serve on social media team and help us make more people aware of this great effort. You can also join a small group online or just share one of our Facebook posts or crusade video clips. View and share these videos at wifijesus.org.

Without the financial support of our partners, none of this could have happened. I could never thank them enough. Hundreds of thousands of dollars have already been spent to get us this far. Our partners are wise investors. We are averaging one new convert for every dollar spent! That is laying up some real treasure in heaven!

If you want to give toward areas like books, Bibles, or to help with crusade costs you can do so at wifijesus.org.

Perhaps you have nothing to give, but you would commit to praying for these givers that God would multiply their gifts back to them for saving a child, redeeming a slave, or purchasing a Bible.

You can also be involved by passing this book on to someone else or by ordering additional copies for your friends at wifijesus.org.

All of these things are a tremendous help in this effort to reach 100 million souls.

Lezli and I have been in ministry long enough now to be strategically placed in three major revolutions. We were in China when the Chinese communist government crushed the revolution for democracy. We were in Eastern Europe when the Iron Curtain fell. Now we are in the middle of a revolution of technology that has forever altered the way people live in every nation. All revolutions offer tremendous windows of opportunity to reach the lost. These are windows that can open and close very quickly. We are in one of those moments right now, and you have the tremendous opportunity to take part in it. Everybody can participate. Join us in this march to reach 100 million souls for Jesus.

Together with the technology that no other prior generation possessed, we can complete the last task the Lord gave us before He ascended into heaven. We can *"Go into all the world and proclaim the gospel to the whole creation"* (Mark 16:15 ESV). Friend, God is calling for His end-time harvest. Don't be put to sleep by what you see happening in the West. The world is starving for hope and hungry for Jesus.

There are many who don't have time for us to delay. One of the next crusades we are doing is in a refugee camp in Uganda. Here is the request from the pastor organizing this video crusade as sent to Pastor Noah:

Shalom in Jesus' name!

I hereby register my appreciation on behalf of all the pastors and leaders who attended the Pastors' Conference that took place in the month of March in Mbarara. We were 25 couples from the refugee camp. Pastor Noah, we pray that God bless you, increase you, anoint you, keep you, and continue to provide for you, for what you did for us!

Our marriages will never remain the same! The teachings of that white man, Pastor Craig on TV, were so awesome, touching, and hope restoring. Tell him we are praying that God bless, protect, and expand his boundaries in God's service!

Pastor Noah our spouses changed; love and joy were restored in our homes. Even though we are refugees in a settlement, our children are experiencing happiness more than ever before. Ministries are changing. We didn't know that a dysfunctional marriage creates a dysfunctional ministry! Our ministries had become dysfunctional, the messages from our pulpits were irrelevant, and instead of edifying they were quarrels because of the squabbles at home. But now! Things are changing for the better.

For your information, Nakivale settlement began around 1958 and officially opened in 1960 because of the war in Rwanda between the Tutsi and Hutu. It has 79 villages and each village has a population of 800–1,000 and sits on an area of 185 km squared. It has a population of 35,000 nationals around it.

It used to host eight nationalities: DR Congolese, Rwandese, Burundians, Somalis, Eritreans, Sudanese, few Liberians, and Kenyans, now it hosts six. The population is 61,000 (2014 census), and DR Congolese dominate the numbers followed by Burundians and Rwandese and then Somalis.

Due to the way of life in the camp, there is too much gender-based violence, even in Christian families, which has resulted in so many deaths and casualties. You visited this camp and you witnessed this yourself. This is a result of dysfunctional homes, and churches, creating dysfunctional societies; and if no prescription and treatment is done for this, then…

Dear Pastor Noah, what plans do you have for us, also as human beings, suffering from lack of food and water, living under tarpaulins, wallowing in poverty, illiteracy; but we are also children of God? Acts 16:9 reminds us; "That night Paul had a vision: A man from Macedonia in northern Greece was standing there pleading with him, 'Come over to Macedonia and help us!'"

And therefore, echoing this Holy Writ, hear the Macedonian man calling from the refugee camp in Western Uganda at the border of Congo, Rwanda, and Tanzania.

We kindly request you to fit us somewhere in your program for an outreach of a video crusade to bring in an end-time harvest and a conference with a marriage workshop to help our fledgling marriages and eventually families.

As refugees living by the mercies of God, it's only in the Word where we find peace, comfort, and solace from our past and present sufferings. We lack the Word of God. You will find like thirty families sharing one Bible. We pray that if God provides, remember us and get us Bibles and Bible study tools.

We have slightly over 29 born-again churches, a pastors' fellowship, and a born-again fraternity, which are capable to organize a very successful meeting to the glory of God and expansion of His Kingdom on earth.

Important to note: If you compare 29 churches with the number of registered refugees with UNHCR and OPM, the harvest is plenty but the harvesters are few! Among the 29 churches, only a quarter of these are the built ones. Many churches fellowship in UNHCR and OPM schools and others under tree shades. Kindly, if God opens the door of assistance, remember us in regards to evangelism, training of leaders, and your church planting program. Someone once said, "If you want to evangelize an area, plant a church!" Let's rest our case here, with a hope that our cry will reach your ears and a positive response be accorded us to the glory of God.

Yours in Him,

Rev. Mwunvirwa Joseph

Pastors Fellowship Representative

NOTE

1. John Stuart Mill, "Inaugural Address Delivered to the University of St. Andrews," February 1, 1867 http://www.notable-quotes.com/m/mill_john_stuart.html.

This is the hunger for God we see across Central Africa.

Ugandan converts giving their lives to Christ during a video crusade.

Never have I witnessed people so hungry for Jesus.

"Those who sit in darkness have seen a great light." Hearing the story of Jesus for the very first time.

Preaching the blood-stained cross of Jesus.

Much of the world is still waiting to hear the greatest story ever told.

Well-worn Bibles are being replaced around the world.

My awesome security team in Pakistan.

Baptizing current slaves in Pakistan in a water trough located on a brick kiln.

This slave's first Bible.

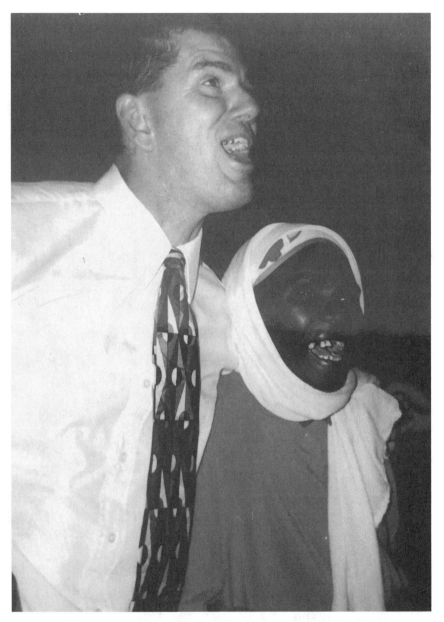

Photo of the paralyzed lady that God miraculously healed in Tanzania during my first crusade.

Photo of Goddess of Democracy taken by our students in Tiananmen Square just prior to the massacre.

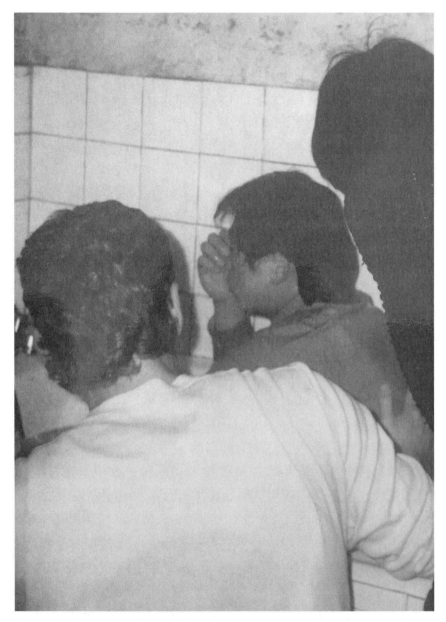

My police translator and dear brother Whitman's baptism in our bathtub.

By all means possible we must take the Gospel to the nations. This is our hour to complete the task!

About Craig Walker

CRAIG WALKER is the author of the books, *Catch: The Art of Fishing for Souls, Secret: The Single Greatest Leadership Key, Taboo: God and Money, Right Message Wrong Method: Church Marketing in a Postmodern World, Forecast: Surviving and Thriving in the Coming Tsunami of Change, Last Minute God,* and *#JOY.*

Pastor Craig speaks and ministers around the world. He and his wife, Lezli, are former missionaries and together have planted churches in China, Czechoslovakia, and America. He is also the founder of Upward Church, WifiJesus.org, and Friends of Internationals Inc.

He is the lead pastor of Upward Church, an online church with physical locations in Norfolk, Virginia; Pensacola, Florida; and Williamsburg, Virginia.

Craig holds a Master's Degree of Theology from International Seminary in Florida. He has been married to his sweetheart, Lezli, for thirty-one years and they have two grown children, Christian and Candace. They currently live in Pensacola, Florida.

For additional information on the Walkers or Upward Church go to: https://www.upwardchurch.org.

An Invitation from Pastor Craig

If you don't have a church, we would love for you to join us at our online campus at upwardchurch.org.

Also, we would love to hear from you. If this book has ministered to you or if you would like additional information, you can reach us at:

Craig.Walker@wifiJesus.org

9859 N Davis Hwy, Pensacola, FL 32514

Facebook: https://www.facebook.com/officialwifijesus/

Facebook: https://www.facebook.com/craig.walker.581

Website: https://www.wifijesus.org/

Website: https://www.upwardchurch.org/

Other Resources by Craig Walker

Last Minute God

Catch: The Art of Fishing for Souls

Secret: The Single Greatest Leadership Key

Taboo: God and Money

Right Message Wrong Method:
Church Marketing in a Postmodern World

Forecast: Surviving and Thriving in the
Coming Tsunami of Change

#JOY.

The Harrison House Vision

Proclaiming the truth and the power
of the Gospel of Jesus Christ with excellence.
Challenging Christians
to live victoriously,
grow spiritually,
know God intimately.

Fast. Easy.
Convenient.

For the latest Harrison House product information and author news, look no further than your computer. All the details on our powerful, life-changing products are just a click away. New releases, email subscriptions, testimonies, monthly specials—find them all in one place. Visit harrisonhouse.com today!

harrisonhouse.com

Connect with us on
[f] Facebook @ HarrisonHousePublishers
and [Instagram] Instagram @ HarrisonHousePublishing
so you can stay up to date with news
about our books and our authors.

Visit us at **www.harrisonhouse.com**
for a complete product listing as well as
monthly specials for wholesale distribution.